SIR WILLIAM BROWNE KNIGHT
1556-1610
AND
SIR NATHANIEL RICH KNIGHT
-1636

A CHAPTER OF
FAMILY HISTORY

by
G. D. Scull

Oxford
1882

Transcription, Notes, and Index by
James W. Brown

HERITAGE BOOKS
2008

HERITAGE BOOKS

AN IMPRINT OF HERITAGE BOOKS, INC.

Books, CDs, and more—Worldwide

For our listing of thousands of titles see our website
at
www.HeritageBooks.com

Published 2008 by
HERITAGE BOOKS, INC.
Publishing Division
100 Railroad Ave. #104
Westminster, Maryland 21157

International Standard Book Numbers
Paperbound: 978-0-7884-4560-6
Clothbound: 978-0-7884-7300-5

Table of Contents

TRANSCRIBER'S NOTES

Browne and Rich, Houses United

The Seventeenth-Century English houses of Browne and Rich were joined by bonds of marriage, class, business, and faith. Although he inherited no title, Percy Browne (1603 - 1635-7), came from the landed gentry of Snelston in Derbyshire. Son of Sir William Browne and Lady Mary (Savage) Browne, Percy married Anne Rich, daughter of Richard Rich and Jane Anne (Machell) Rich. Percy Browne and his siblings were born in the Netherlands where their soldier father Sir William was long stationed as Lieutenant-Governor of Flushing (Vlissingen). Those children who came of age were naturalized as citizens of England by separate acts of Parliament, as was their mother Mary, a European by birth, and a commoner. Sir William's mother, Eleanor Shirley, counted kings and emperors in her long pedigree, and Sir William himself was knighted by Queen Elizabeth. Sir William's son Percy married into the Rich family, thus bringing together the houses of Rich and Browne, and their children subsequently took leading roles in the westward expansion to the Atlantic Islands and the American mainland. Robert Browne, Percy's son and a Puritan minister at Bermuda, inherited a share in the Bermuda Company from his uncle Nathaniel Rich and another share from his widowed mother, Nathaniel's sister Margaret (Rich) Roth. Robert Browne's brother Nathaniel emigrated to Connecticut in 1633 under the patronage of the firebrand Puritan Reverend Thomas Hooker, and there fathered the beginnings of a pious Connecticut dynasty. I may parenthetically add that one of Rev. Robert's Browne's sons, Abell, found his way to Maryland, where he and his descendants participated in the establishment of that colony. Evidence also suggests that the family was somehow connected to the Brownes of Surrey County's Beechworth Castle and its resident baronetcy.

The Riches shone amongst England's Tudor aristocracy. They included the Barons Rich and Kensington and the Earls of Warwick and Holland. Henry Rich, Earl of Holland, Robert Rich, Second Earl of Warwick, and others of the family were notable figures in English politics and literature. Robert Rich, whose poetic narrative recounted his shipwreck and hardships on Bermuda, is widely said to have inspired Shakespeare's *Tempest*. (The reader is advised to consult Mr. Jacobus' account of the Rich family pedigree, as it differs from Scull's.) Sir Nathaniel Rich was a determined investor in England's Atlantic colonial enterprise, the avowed purposes of which were to make money and to spread the Puritan Protestant faith. Both Sir Nathaniel Rich and Sir William Browne were shareholders and co-signers of the Virginia Company's Second Charter, and it was Sir Nathaniel who played a leading role in the colonization of Bermuda (then known as the Sommers or Somers Islands) and the Providence Islands, the latter a Puritan stronghold until that colony's capture by the Spaniards in 1641. Until his death in 1636, Sir Nathaniel served on the governing board of the Bermuda Company, which operated from its London base. Such is the backdrop of G.D. Scull's informative manuscript.

G. D. Scull, Expatriate Man of Letters

There is little about Gideon Delaplaine Scull's quiet life to excite the biographical urge. For the present it is enough to say that he was born on 13 August 1824 in Sculltown (or Auburn) New Jersey, of a family that was engaged in the woolen trade; that he studied at Haverford College; worked in and retired from the family business, as his health was not robust; emigrated to England; married Anna Holder of Warwick on 7 April 1862, had two children, Walter and Edith; lived for some time in Oxford; traveled widely and devoted himself to study and writing; and died in Ilkey, Yorkshire on 22 April 1889 at the age of 65. That seems to be about all.

Nevertheless, he left behind a respectable *corpus* of scholarly editions, historical studies and genealogies. Perhaps best known is his *Voyages of Peter Esprit Radisson* (Boston, 1885), taken from the explorer's journals that Scull came upon in the Bodleian Library at Oxford. Other works of that "expatriate man of letters," as he was once called, include *The Montressor Journals* (1882), *Journal of the Siege of York-town*, *Scull Family of Pennsylvania*, *Genealogical Notes Relating to the Family of Scull* (1876), *Evelyns in America*, and *Memoirs and Letters of Captain W. Glanville Evelyn* (1879), plus numerous articles and poetry, as well as the study presented here.

It was during one of his several trips back to his native land that Scull presented in 1882 the manuscript entitled *Sir William Browne, Knight, 1556-1610, and Sir Nathaniel Rich, Knight, -1636: A Chapter of Family History* to the New England Historic Genealogical Society, where it remains. A letter of query to the Society (of which Scull was a corresponding member) had raised the possibility that certain Browns of America were descended from a Lord-Mayor of London, and that manuscript was his response. It appears that his investigation of the

3

Browne saga led him to a conjoined study of the Riches, because the two families' stories and fortunes were so finely intertwined.

The often meandering manuscript presents key episodes of both family histories, primarily through their letters and documents, with Scull's comments and explanations. They include William Browne's account of the disastrous fleet expedition toward Ireland against the threatening Spanish, Browne's duties and perils while serving in Elizabeth's protracted Low Country campaign, plus an account of his family and nearer descendants. Of the Rich family Scull details Sir Nathaniel Rich's efforts in support of Britain's Atlantic colonies, and in Parliament his long and perilous struggle to defend that body's rights before the overweening First Kings James and Charles. Then Scull passes to the soldier-explorer Robert Rich and his historic shipwreck at Bermuda, thence to Robert's son Colonel Nathaniel Rich, who fought honorably for Cromwell in the British Civil War, but later fell from grace as a member of the Fifth Monarchist sect. Following that, Scull returns to Sir Nathaniel and reviews his will, which gives an opportunity to parade out, in no apparent order, that leading figure's many relatives and acquaintances. Only then does Scull take up the question, but offers no conclusion, of the Brownes' possible descent from Sir Stephen Browne, Lord Mayor of London, and with that he outlines the conjoined Rich family history. Finally, in a coda of sorts, Scull offers up Robert Rich's verses that reputedly inspired Shakespeare's *Tempest*. Although the poem describes Bermuda as an "Iland of deuils," *Newes from Virginia* goes on to make an impassioned call to further emigration to the overseas colonies. Scull then appends the "Grant of Arms to the Summer Islands Company" of 1635, and so ends the manuscript.

As he wrote, Scull was unaware that a contemporary, the barrister and historian John Pym Yeatman, was also investigating the Brownes in Derbyshire and elsewhere. It is equally clear that Pym Yeatman had no knowledge of Scull's efforts, and so it is instructive to compare them. While both made valuable contributions to the family's history by using the sources each had at hand, the contrast in their grander assertions may serve as cautionary to the researcher. On the one hand, Scull detailed Sir William Browne's long service to his country and the several honors granted him and his widow. On the other hand Pym Yeatman, depending on local sources with a confusion of Brownes, and drawing a shaky analogy with the fate of some Catholic Brownes he believed to be (and probably were) cousins, declared that Sir William Browne had fled from Queen Elizabeth and England as a recusant Papist, settled in the Low Countries "where he could at least fight," and crept back years later, humbled and broken. Scull's less ambitious but well-buttressed study presented here is far the more persuasive. (Both Scull and Pym Yeatman erred in estimating Sir William Browne's actual date of death. It was on 9 April 1811, as witnessed and described in a letter from Mr. R. Taverner to William Trumbull, English ambassador to the Netherlands.) It is quite evident that Scull enjoyed access to privately owned archives, those of the Sidney and Dudley families, and perhaps others that have not been identified.

Indeed, as he briefly believed himself accused of disloyalty, Browne's frantic and frankly groveling 1601 letter to the Queen's Privy Council came inserted into Scull's manuscript and is shown here. It gives every evidence of being the original letter. How Scull obtained that document and why he inserted it into his study will here pass without speculation.

Although for the most part factually good, Scull's style and organization give evidence of both idiosyncrasy and haste, the result of which I have left intact. I shall only comment that in the Sir Anthony Browne family chart, he left unfinished a sentence indicating the extinction year of the Browne Betchworth (Beechworth) Castle baronetcy. For the record, that year was given in Burke's *Extinct Baronetage* as 1690.

Special thanks go to the New England Historic Genealogical Society's R. Stanton Avery Special Collections Department for its courtesy and cooperation.

Some terms that may not be readily understood are:

adelantado - (Sp. naut.) fleet commander
adventure - investment
adventurer - investor
antimonial cupp - (med.) antimony added to wine as an emetic or
    purgative
bedroll (beadroll) - published church list of persons needful of prayer
beare - (bear, bere) pillow cover
betten - beaten
Bristow - Bristol
caltroppe - (mil.) caltrop, multipronged spike scattered to pierce horses'
    hooves
carract - (Sp. *carraca*) sailing ship used for freight
clister - (med.) clyster, enema
Cowes - city in Isle of Wight
crased - (crazed), unsound, in poor condition
David's example - as expressed in his Psalms, trusting to one's faith in
    God in times of distress
deale boards - deals, planks
debare - (debar) restrain
drum - (mil.) messenger
Eijsden - Eisden, city in Limburger, Belgium
ffeeoffee - (feoffee) freehold trustee or owner of a feudal estate or fief
fferme - (ferme, ferm) rent, lease

fishes - (naut.) fish plates, connecting plates
garboyle - garboil, disturbance
groyne - ("The Groyn") La Coruña, Galicia's major port and the
    Armada's stopping-off en route to and from the north; hence, "the
    land of the Groyne" = Spain
Isendick - Ijzendijke, town in Zeeland
king at arms - senior heraldic official
king's evil - scrofula, so called because of the belief that a king's touch
    would cure it
last - group, batch (falcons)
Margett - Margate, Kent
maugre - (Fr. *malgré*) in spite of
mickle - much, great
miscen - (naut.) mizzen
nolens volens - (Lat.) willingly or unwillingly
partners - (naut.) paired timbers that support a mast
pharol - (Sp., Por. *farol*) lighthouse
pike - pick, draw out, i.e., a compliment
pinace - (naut.) pinnace, a small sailing craft
pylotte - pilot
quondam = (Lat.) formerly known as
robe - (of the long robe) of the legal profession
roomer - (naut.) under full sail
senight - se'nnight, week
Skute - Schoten, city in Belgium
Sloue - Slough, city west of London
Sluce - Sluis, city south of Vlissingen
Stonton - Stondon Massey, village near Brentwood in Essex
sudain, sodain - emergency
surprise - act of treachery, ambush
torce - wreath
towled - (tolled) paid
triumph - (v.) to celebrate

Suggestions for further reading:

Brown, James W. *Browne - Brown Descendants of England, West Indies,
    Maryland, New England and the American Frontier.*
    Westminster MD: Willow Bend, 2006.
Browne Letters Collection. Centre for Kentish Studies on Behalf of the
    Viscount De L'Isle. Maidstone, Kent.
Collins, Arthur, ed. *Letters and Memorials of State.* Sidney family

papers. 2 vols. London: Osborne (1746), 1973.

Hollis Hallett, A. C. *Early Bermuda Records 1619-1826*. Bermuda: Juniperhill Press, 1991.

Ives, V. A., ed. *The Rich Papers: Letters from Bermuda 1615-1646*. Bermuda: Bermuda National Trust, 1984.

Jacobus, Donald Lines "The House of Rich." *The American Genealogist,* 21 (1944), 234-8; 22 (1945), 27-37, 157-165, 240-8; 23 (1946), 101-9.

Potts, W., and J. W. Dean. "[Necrology of] Gideon Delaplaine Scull," *New England Historical and Genealogical Register*, 45 (Oct. 1891), 324-6.

Pym Yeatman, John. *The Brownes of Bechworth Castle*. [London]: Published by the author, 1903.

_____. "The Brownes of Snelston." Vol. 4, Sect. 7, of *The Feudal History of the County of Derby*, 6 Vols. London: Bemrose, ca 1886-1908.

Waters, Henry F. "Sir Nathaniel Rich." In the series "Genealogical Gleanings in England," *New England Historical and Genealogical Register*, 48 (April 1894), 267-70. Reprinted in Genealogical *Gleanings in England,* Vol. II. (1981), 871-874.

James W. Brown

Preface

This little volume of family history owes its origin to the following query inserted in the January Number (1882) of the New England Historical and Genealogical Register —

"Brown. "Brown" was one of the earliest settlers at Ipswich hamlet, now Hamilton, where he owned a large tract of land and as his sons, of whom he had ten, successfully reached the age of 21 years he gave each a farm, reserving the homestead for his youngest son Stephen, from whom we are descended. I can only ascertain the names of eight of the sons, viz - Nathaniel, John - Simon - Adam - James - Thomas - Jacob - and Stephen. -

There was always a tradition in the family that they were descendants of Sir Stephen Brown, an English Baronet. It is said that Stephen sold the homestead, and invested the money in a Ship which he commanded. He afterwards resided in Charleston, where he married Mary Barrow, said to have been a considerable heiress. Squire Brown, as he was called, a brother of the old gentleman, lived next the church in Wenham, a man of note, very much respected and very wealthy; had no children. At his death his property was divided amongst the families of Brown, with whom he was connected, of whom there were many.

One of the family married a Story, who went to live in Mississippi and was in Excellent circumstances. He came with his wife to visit his relatives at Wenham. I wish to know who were the progenitors in England, and with what families of Brown they are connected in this country."

Boston —   M. B. Pratt

It is hoped that the publication of this little volume of the Browne family history in England will be the means of stimulating some of the members of this now somewhat numerous Sept in the United States and to all the descendants of the ten Sons of Nathaniel Browne, the original progenitor in New England.

Rugby Lodge, Norham Road
Oxford, August 28th, 1882   G. D. Scull

Sir William Browne Knt.

Queen Elizabeth had been for some time secretly endeavouring by means of money to counteract the designs of the King of Spain in the Low Countries, but in 1585 she was forced to adopt a more open practice and sent over a royal army of 6000 men, so acting as a condition that the States were to pay all her expenses and deliver to her as securities the towns of Brill & Flushing and the strong fort of Rammekins. These were called the Cautionary towns. The Earl of Leicester, uncle to Sir Philip Sydney was appointed to command the forces. Sir Philip was also with the troops, as well as his younger brother Robert, who arrived at Flushing two days after his uncle, and in time to take part in an engagement before the town. For his valour, on this occasion he was knighted by the Earl of Leicester 7th Octr 1586 and on the 16th July 1588 made Lord Governor of Flushing. Sir Phillip had up to his death at Zutphen held this appointment and had as an officer under him, one Captain William Browne the only son of a country gentleman of Derbyshire. Arthur Collins, the Editor of the "Sydney papers" says of Captain Browne "he had served from the breaking out of the wars in the Low Countries and was much valued by Sir Phillip Sydney who intrusted him with the Enterprize of the Surprize of Graveline, anno 1586, where by Treachery he was taken prisoner. After signalising himself in several other actions he was made Lieutenant Governor of Flushing in which post he died leaving the reputation of a brave and Experienced Commander." Collins adds the following note "For the leadership in the Surprise of Graveline Sir Philip Sydney not wishing to hazard the lives of many gentlemen, made the inferior officers try their fortune by Dice on a Drumhead. The lot fell on Captain William Browne, his own Lieutenant, who with a choice company presently departed receiving this provisional caution from Sir Philip, that if he found Practice and not faith he should throw down his arms and yield himself prisoner, protesting that if they took him he should be ransomed and if they broke Quarter his death most severely revenged. The leader following his General's Commandment discovers the Treachery, throws Down his Arms and is taken prisoner, and its agreed that Sir Philip's penetration and judgment saved the lives and Honour of the English Army by not hazarding so many of them in that treacherous expedition. During the protracted absence of Sir Robert Sydney in Holland, for the Queen would not give him long leaves of absence, and very few of them, he was regularly supplied with news of a public and a private character, by Rowland Whyte, a very worthy man, and most reliable correspondent, who was employed by Sir Robert on a salary to act as his solicitor at Court. Roland Whyte was also a friend and correspondent of Captain Browne, and when the Lieu' Governor of Flushing, Sir Edward Uvedale absented himself for some time in England, and was detained there by his private business and also by illness, a timely word of advice by Whyte, in the proper quarter secured for his friend in Holland, the deputyship of this post as locum tenens, which eventually led to his appointment as Lieu' Governor. Roland Whyte 19th December 1595, writes to Sir Robert Sydney that "Mr Lake sent unto me from Sir Robert Cecil to know, who your Lordship wold leave in your place, now that Sir Edward Uvedale was here, I sent him this word, that the charge of the town you wold be most carefull of. That you had in the Town at this houre Captain Browne, a Gentleman your Lordship Knew to be discreet, valiant, well affected in Religion, well languaged and one that was specially well acquainted with the Humours of the Burgesses and mariners and every way such a one as your Lordship wold be answerable for." Captain Browne obtained the post of Lieutenant Governor of Flushing in the latter end of the reign of Queen Elizabeth, and held it with honour and dignity until his death in August 1610. The honour of knighthood was conferred on him by the Queen in 1597. He was married some little time before 1599 as the following entry proves, and which is Extracted from the State paper office "January 27th 1600 — Grant of free denization to Mary Savage born in Germany, now wife to Sir William Browne." By Germany is no doubt meant Belgium, as in "1623 April 6th Letters of safe conduct for Lady Mary Browne of Ghent denizen of England to go abroad for three years." A letter from Flushing August 10, 1610 alludes to the illness of Sir Wm Browne, which obliges John Throckmorton to write in his stead. He succeeded him as Lieut Governor. King James I recognized his services to the state in the following paper "In consideration of the good and acceptable services done unto us and to our crowne of England by our late trusty and well beloved Sir William Browne Knight, deceased Lieutenant Governor of our cautionary Town of Flushing and for other causes and consideration moving us hereunto, we are pleased for the better maintenance and education of his children to bestow upon the Lady Browne late wife to the said Sir William Browne, an annuity or Pention of One hundred Markes by the yeare, to be taken to her for the uses aforesaid out of such moneys as from tyme to tyme doe accrew unto us by the Cheques rising out of the entertaynement and apparrelling of the soldiers of that our Garrison of fflushing. Payment to be half yearly and to begin at the Feast of St Michael the Archangell next coming after date hereof (20 July 1611) for Lady Browne's natural life. To Richard

Wright Esq. paymaster of the Forces in the Low Countries."—[φ] On the 1st of June 1604 a bill was read for the first time in the House of Commons for naturalizing the children of Sir William Browne L[t] Gov[r] of Flushing viz William – Ann – and Barbara Browne." The bill was read a third time, and passed 22 June 1604. In the will of Sir William Browne it is required of the Trustees that his children shall be naturalized in England. Accordingly we find that on June 22[d] 1622 there was a "grant to Percy and Mary Browne children of the late Sir William Browne Lieutenant of Flushing and borne there, of denization." These two children Percy and Mary, alone survived, and had for their Trustees six friends of their father viz — Sir William Russell Knight, Sir Robert Sydney Knight, Peter Morwood Esq[r], Thomas Edmonds Esq[r], Rowland Whyte and Philip Harrison. In the will of Sir Nathaniel Rich made in 1635, he mentions four of his nephews, sons of his deceased sister Browne, and one of them "—— Browne, one other of the sons of my sister Browne deceased, who hath been hitherto educated by my noble ffriend the Countefs of Leicester, Mother of Sir John Smith." This Sir John Smith married Lady Isabel Rich daughter of Rob[t] Rich 1st Earl of Warwick and Penelope. This Countefs of Leicester was Sarah daughter & heiress of W[m] Blount, and became the 3rd wife of Sir Thomas Smyth, who died in 1625. Sir

---

[φ] In 1616 King James 1st Received £13.000 Extra dividend from the States General over and above of the stipulated sum of £200.000 for the delivering up of the Cautionary towns Flushing, Zealand and Brill to the Dutch. This £13.000 was divided amongst the officers, office holders &[c] and Lady Browne was paid £300 at Brill as a recognition of her husband Sir William Browne's services to the State as Lieutenant Governor of Flushing.

14

Thomas was closely identified with the schemes of colonization of Virginia and the West India Islands particularly the Summers and Providence group in which Sir Nathaniel Rich was also interested. After the death of Sir Thomas, his widow married in 1626 to Sir Robert Sydney who however died a few months after in 1626. Sir Robert some little time before his death succeeded his uncle, and became 1st Earl of Leicester of the name of Sydney. In the will of Sir Nathl Rich he seems not to have known the Christian name of the nephew who was educated by his "ffriend the Countess of Leicester" but it was in all probability William, for in a letter to Captain Nathaniel Butler Governor, dated June 7 - 1639, and Business of the Company of Providence Island it is mentioned that "Will Browne and Ed Tuston who have been condemned to death, to have their liberty but not allowed to leave the island." Of the other sons of the "deceased sister Browne" he gives to Nathaniel Browne now in New England with Mr Hooker the Two hundred pounds which by my sister Morgan's will was bequeathed unto him and ffifty pounds more as my own Guift." He also gives "one other share of the Somers Island Company to my nephew Robert Browne now residing in the said Somers Island he having one other share there already upon the guift of my Sister Wroth lately deceased. No mention is made of the other nephew having been sent out of England. He was probably too young, and remained to complete his education. There was a Samuel Browne, who eventually became one of the six clerks of the Chancery, and rose to be one of the King's Bench, and knighted. Sir Nathaniel Rich left to his nephew Samuel Browne £100, "the same to be employed during his minority for his benefit." —

Of the Six Trustees named in Sir William Browne's will, Sir Robert Sydney and Rowland White would naturally of them all become practically, the guardians in England of young Percy Browne. He was

15

naturalized in 1622 and we may afsume that he was then of age, and married soon after. Nathaniel was probably his eldest son, and Robert perhaps was born in 1626, the year of Sir Robert Sydney's death, and named after him. Both Percy Browne and his wife were deceased at the date of Sir Nathaniel Rich's will, 1635. It would seem that Sir Nathaniel had taken charge of three of the four sons of his deceased "Sister Browne" and that the fourth was educated by the Countess of Leicester, the widow of Sir Robert Sydney. Robert Browne became a clergyman, in the Somer's Islands, having been appointed a minister there in 1655, and died in 1661.

The property of the Browne family at Snelston, Derbyshire, seems to have been sold some time between 1611 and 1662, as a pedigree appears of the family in the visitation of the County in 1611, and is absent when another was made by Dugdale in 1662/3.

It would seem that Percy Browne did not reside on his estate at Snelston, at the time of his death, for neither his name or his wife's, occur in the parish register of his church, nor can his will, or his wife's be found in the probate court at Lichfield.

Whilst Sir Robert Sydney was absent from England, we have seen that he was kept well informed of passing events at home by his indefatigable correspondent Rowland Whyte; and when he was absent from his post, on leave in England Cap^{tn} William Browne was not a whit less industrious and attentive in supplying him, as he was bound to do, as his deputy, with information concerning affairs in Holland. From first to last, Cap^{tn} Browne wrote to the Lord General of Flushing about 130 letters which have been preserved among the family papers of the Sydneys at Penshurst. Besides these, there are extant 30 addressed to Sir Robert Cecil and 2 to the Earl of Essex, in the possession of the Marquiss of Salisbury. Those to the Earl of Essex are dated respectively Jany 7th &

16

25th - 1598. The letters addressed to Sir Robert Sydney are mostly filled with descriptions of skirmishes and battles, the movements of troops the state of the garrison at Flushing and political affairs in the States General, but much can be gleaned here and there from them, to show what mutual confidence and affection existed between Sir Rob[t] Sydney and the writer. Selections will therefore be made from the correspondence, of whatever is of personal and historical interest.

The first letter from Capt[n] Browne to Sir Rob[t], who had returned to England on leave of absence is from Flushing 14th Aug[t] 1596 and the last (that has been published in the Collection of the Sydney Papers in 2 vol[s], edited by Arthur Collins in 1746.) is dated 12 of March 1610. It may be remembered that Sir William died in the month of August of that year, and was succeeded by Sir John Throckmorton. .. From the following letter addrefsed by Sir Thomas Bodley to Sir Robert Sydney, it would appear that Cap[t] Browne was desirous of going with his Company to France, as there was some prospect of his seeing service abroad. Sir Thomas Bodley was actively employed by Queen Eliz[th] for some years, as her political and businefs agent & envoy in the Low Countries. "From the Hage Sep[t] 16th 1592 "I hope that Cap[t] Browne hath received my Letter & is satisfied fully of my affection to his suite, if it lay in my power. There are 4 of the Companies of your garrison required by name to be shipped for France, of which his is one." Whilst Sir Rob[t] was out of England Lady Sydney gave birth (on the 1st Dec[r] 1595) to a son. She had caught the measles, and when the child was born, his body was quite covered with the eruptions. The child, however thrived, and at Lady Rich's (the famous Penelope Rich) especial request, he was to be called Robert. She, Lord Mountjoy, and Lord Compton, were named the Sponsors and Rowland Whyte writes the 22nd of February (1596) "This day senight is the christening and my Lady desires Captain Browne to

17

stay his journey to the Country till it be past, for she will use his service here that day. All the great Ladys, her neighbors, doe bid themselves unto it." The christening was fixed for the 29th of Feby and on the 28th Sir Robert was informed that "Sir Mathew Morgan, Captains Browne, Barry, Morison and Burnham will be tomorrow to attend the great Ladies at Savoye." On the Day of Ceremony (Whyte informs Sir Robert) "the Captens of Flushing were their alone and they had all things prepared and necessary for their calling." It is also stated that the sponsors "gave three very fair standing Bowles, all of one Fashion, worth 20 £ each." In July of the next year we find Capt Browne and a number of the officers from the garrison at Flushing, at Plymouth ready to accompany the Earl of Essex, on an expedition against the Spaniards. Philip the 2nd had resolved to make an effort against Ireland, of which the Queen had timely notice, and had planned this movement to Counteract it. But contrary winds, storms and a quarrel which broke out between the Earl of Essex and Sir Walter Rawleigh prevented these measures from taking effect, and the fleet returned to Plymouth, as Capt William Browne mentions in his letters. In addition to the Commanders of the 3 Squadrons, Lord Mountjoy was the general of the land forces, which consisted of 6000 men. A fleet of 3 score vessels was equipped for the Expedition. With the land forces Sir Francis Vere acted as Marshal de Camp.

My most honored good Lord

I will briefly write our Adventure unto you since our putting to sea from Plimouth, which was on Sunday the 10th of July. We sailed prosperously enough till the next Day at Esen, when we felt a Contrary Wind and Overblowing. The Order of our going out was in 3 Squadrons, my Lord Essex, my Lord Thomas Howard, Vice Admirall, and Sir Walter Rawley, Rere admirall: amongst these three wer all our Fleet dispensed: On the Monday Night, Sir Walter Rawley left us, and divers of his Squadron in his Company: we sailed all the rest of us in reasonable good Order, neare the Generall, althoghe the Wether was extreme: but our Shipp, being the Mary Rose, not the swiftest of Saile, nor the Best of Stearage and having darke stormy Wether, lost my Lord General on Friday after being the 15th of July: and wee beatt about against the Wind till Sunday after, butt cold not recover Sight of our Generall: and on the Same Sunday we were driven to goe back before the Wind, having spent our maine Mast, I meane, having so crased with bearing Saile in both the Partners that all her Fishes were broken round about and if she had broken there, we had endangered our Ship, which besides had a great Leake: but we made such Shifts, as with Anker Stock we fished her so well, as that she was able to bring us Home to Plimouth, where we arrived on Tuesday after, and found come in the Day before Sir Walter Rawley, and the Bonaventure. There came in with the two Spanish Ships, the Suresyght, and the Drednaught. A Day after landed my Lord General at Farmouth, he came from thence by Land, whose Daunger, how great itt was, both through his Leake springing, his miscen Mast, and maine Bolts, with Beames wrought out and shaken, you shall have generall Newes of Som Shipps, of Soldiours as likewise retourned hither, amonge the rest Jack Sidney with a rotten Flieboat, was in Daunger to be drowned, and was driven back to Avonsmouth, and came hither, and is this Day retourned to make Hast with his Men hither, where he shall have other Shipping if he Com in Time, becaus my Lord is determined to putt out Tomorrow, if the Winds hold: for the most Part of our Forces they Keepe the Sea still, for any Thing we can learne. The Spanish Navy hath bene at Sea, and, as itt is reputed, Sett out the same Day that my Lord Generall did, and the same foule Wether that hindred us, drove him into Harbour into Pharol, being alredy the first Wind to putt out, we have certen Newes of Sicknes, and Want of Vittaills in his Army: there is a

Prize or two Comme in hither that hath taken Wine, it was for the Navy, better wirth then 1500 £. We are heare 8 of the Quenes Shipps, the Marioner, where my Lord went, and shall now be left behind us: the Lyon is sent for him, but he is determined to leave Order that she shall follow, and he will putt himself, with som Small Traine, in the Bonaventure, which is likewise heare, as also the Warspryte: the Mary Rose, the Dreadnought, the Foresygt, the 2 Spanish Shipps, called the Andrew, and the Mathew. I can write little of our Purpose, as being a Thinge rather gefsed att yett then knowne, and yett, in Brief, those that know somewhat, think we shall rather, as we are now, sustaine a Skorne then do any Good: I write to your Lordship plainly my Conceit of your Frend heare, I think he remembers yow not so much as I cold wish, butt itt maybe his owne Busines presseth him too much: butt my Lord of Rutland often honereth mee, and in most effectionate kind sort speakes of you, and hath that honerable Conceit of your worth as I wold thinke he scarse cold have thoght uppon in these Yeares. This Day being Sunday the 24th of July, we are to go out, as my Lord did yesterday determine: he hath yett received no Answer from the Court: Sir Tho Gates went hether from my Lord, and itt is thoght, if itt Com not very speedily he will make Hast, least a Command shold Com to stay him. We shall leave divers of our Land Soldiors behind us, and putt the rest, I thinke into such Shipes as be nimble of Saile, able to Keep Company with the Queenes Ships, and, I think unless we see we can beat there Fleat, we shall land no Men. There Adelantado is for certen resolved, either to attend us, or to Comme to us, and if we find not the other 8 Ships, that be with my Lord Thomas, in very good Case to fight, God knowes whether we shal be able to do him any Harme: Butt of this enough, and I fear to much: if my letter shold happen into straunge Hands, althogh I write nothing, butt that, which if I were worthy to bee tasked, I wold speake to our Generall, and wold thinke I shold be thoght both honest, and to honor him in saying so much, butt itt may be, he hath som other surer Plott then we can conjecture, which God grant, that his too much forwardness to pursue his Countreys Enemies do not endaunger so worthy a stay of our Common Wealth. Myself am determined to follow him to the last. This in Hast. From Plimmouth this 24 July 1597. Your Lordships most faithful follower   william Browne

P.S. There are Rumours, that the Boatts, where Capten Brett, Capten Budley and Austin Heath were, shold be all three drowned: It is Certen that som Shipps with Soldiors have bene spoken with at Sea being in great Distress butt we hope the best: we heare that Sir Antony Shirley is landed at Cowes, and his Ship goeth to Bristow, and he goes to London, but we say heare very poore: Sir Richd Ruddale was yesterday buried here, being dead of Sea Sickness: this Storm hath killed the Harts of many voluntary Gentlemen, who are retourned already from Plimmouth: my selfe, if please God I retorne in Safety, wil be a continuall Follower of yours, in the Charge which I have there by your honorable Favour. Arthur Champernon goeth in a little Bark of his owne this Jorney, as neatt as himself and the Shipp for Burden, as little as he for a man.

My most honorable good Lord

In my other Letter, whereof likewise this Bearer, Mr Gilpin, is the Bringer, I writt unto you, that my Lord Generall on Sunday last shold putt to Sea, butt the uncerteties are so great, and the Wind so inconstant, that we can build uppon no Resolution taken over Night. You hear, I doubt not, by others, that divers of our Foote Companies are discharged, generally all the armed men sent back, butt most of there Armes caried along: Sir Ferdinando Gorge goeth not: my Lord Generall hath laine these 2 last Nights on Board. Yesterday, being the 28th came in my Lord of Cumberlands Pinefs, who, with the Moone, was sent out on Sunday last to find the Fleat, butt were driven back by foule Wether, and the Moone is putt into Farmouth: Jack Sydney is not yett comme to us from Warmouth. We have, since my last, herd nothing of our Fleet, but the Advyse, a Piness, which was sent out on Saturday last, as itt is thoght, hath gotten upp unto them. Sir Antony Shirley is heare, and goeth the Voiage as it is said, he promiseth great Welth with few Shipps: but for the Honor of my Lord of Essex, many are already wery of this Jorney. I am resolved to stay to see the last Man borne, att my Retorne to dispose wholy of my self as you shall appoint. Two Nights past I supped with Sir Robt Mansfield, where was very good Company, my Lord Burgh, Sir Th. Germin, Sir Sam. Bagnal, Sir Antony Luck, Mr Somersett Fatt Garrett, Sir Th^o Knowles Mr Grevill, Mr Robt Knowles, and many other: where Mr Robt Knowles druncke to me your Health, which went the Round with most exceeding kind Remembrance. Cary Renolds is faln sick, and I think goes no more: my Lord Ritch thoghe once he was resolved to go, now as itt seems, is in a Dout what to do: I pray God send us a Prosperous Wind, that we may see the Events of our Expectations: And thus having nothing else at this Instant to write I humbly take my Leave of your Honor to whom, as likewise to my good Lady and your Children, I wish all Happines. From Plimmouth this XXIXth of July 1597. Your Honors &c &c William Browne

My most honorable good Lord.

Since my other two (which likewise you shall receive by Mr Gilpin) the rest of our Fleat is arrived hear at Plimmouth & have bene within sight of the Land of the Groyne, where the Advyse came to them & gave them Knowledg of my Lords Putting back into Plimmouth: she came to them on Wednesday last, at night, & on Thursday they came roomer for England, they arrived heare on this Sunday Morning, by 4 of

22

the Clock, being the Last of July: God be thanked they be all in better Case than we Expected, having beaten itt out this fowle wether against the Wind, & no Ship of Soldiours missing: & I think that they are the most of them in so good Estate, as that we shal be redy to take the first prosperous Wind. The King of Spaynes Fleat lies still in Harbor, our Fleat met with some of them, butt they had no Wind to comme out: we begin to have now very good fresh hope of our Journey, which God graunts. If I had thoght that my former Letter shold no sooner have come unto you, I wold rather have sent them by way of London. My Lord Generall goeth now in the Repulse, where he was the last year, & my Lord Thomas in the Bonaventure, as itt is said. Thus having no other Thing to write at this Time, I must humbly take my Leave in hast. From Plimmouth the Last of July 1597

Your Lordshipps most faithfull Follower for ever Wm Browne.

My most honored good Lord — Since my other three, my Lord of Essex went on Monday, last up to the Court, to sollicite the thorough Dispatch that somewhat may yett be effected: my Lord of Southampton is likewise gone after him Butt to retorne, my Lord Warden, Sir Walter Rawley, is gone with my Lord Generall. The Lord Monjoy, the Lord Th^o Howard & my Lord marshall are left to governe Matters: our Soldiours are most on Land dispersed into divers Villages, butt carry their meat with them from off of Shipboard: all are Known to be safe, unless itt be Capt Berry, of whom as yett we have nothing what shold be becomme of him butt we dont know of his Safty. Hear Desiring, not to lett any Thinge passe, worthy of your Knowledg without advertising your Honor I humbly take leave. Plimmouth this 3. August 1597. Wm Browne

Concerning this Expedition of the Earl of Essex, complaints were made that Sir Robt Sydney Allowed so many officers to leave Flushing to accompany him. It must have been on the return of these officers, through London, on their way back to the Low Countries that Captain Browne was knighted by Queen Elizabeth. On the 28th October 1597 she made 9 knights viz —Egerton, Arthur Gorge, Vavasour, Fulke, Greville, William Browne, Harry Dockrey and others, all of whom were from the garrison of Flushing. Sir Robert Sydney procured a short leave of absence, and on his return he was made joint commander with Sir Francis Vere, over the English Auxiliary forces in Holland. In 1599, we find him making great exertions to induce the Queen to recall him, who seemed determined that he should remain. Finding the Governor so anxious to rejoin his family, Sir William Browne went over to England and actively employed himself about the Court for some time in endeavouring to procure the much desired leave for his Chief. Rowland Whyte, had a special interview with the Earl of Essex, and secured his friendly promise of aid, and how industriously Sir W[m] worked is told by Whyte — 20. October 1599 — "Touching your leave to return I moved Sir Robert Cecil about y[t] at Court. xxxx. Sir W[m] Browne is here a good solicitor about y[t] and as sone as he hath Kissed the Queen's hand and effected your license, he will away, for he will not goe into the country though many cawses move hym to doe yt for his own private Busines because he swore he wold not absent hymself here hence to be a Hindrence to your Leave which truly he Performs and findes himself infinitely bownd unto you for many Kynd Favors he receves here at your honorable Frend's Hands. He doth you all the Honor he can devise in all places and companies that he is in — Believe me, he is unto you, an right honest and a faithful Frend and Follower, which in these Dayes are hard to be found." A few days later 25 October "Sir William Browne doth honestly and willingly follow this your Leave to M[r] Secretary who wold have hym attend my Lord Admiral (Essex) about y[t] and he wold second hym: my Lord Admiral protested to Sir William he wold doe yt and that

24

next to his own children, he most respected and loved you and your children. I see Sir William Browne makes this one of his Chieftest Busines at Court which I give way for hym to doe but I accompany hym and assist hym in y^t." The efforts of Sir Wm Browne prove to be of no avail, and he is about to return. Whyte writes – 13 Nov^r (1599) "Mr Secretary (Cecil) remembers his Promis and my Lord Admiral, unto you, and will answer nothing but that he will write himself unto you by Sir William Browne." Before returning Sir W^m leaves the matter in the hands of an able & willing ally the Countess of Warwick (Lady Rich) as Whyte informs us — 16 March 1599/1600 — "My Lady Warwick coming from the Queen told me, that her Majestie will beg her signifie her Pleasure unto you, and with all told her, that she might be assured it shuld be nothing to discontent you: and by Francke, her Ladyship meanes to send it unto you. Mr Secretary also returning from the Queen to his Chamber, called me unto him and said "By G— I moved the Queen for Sir Robt Sydney's Return: She was angry with me for it and will not lett him come over. I know not how others may prevaile: her Majestie is angry also at him for seeking it." I know this will very much discontent my Lady who was in Hope to have seen you by Easter or very shortly after. She will surely come to court and kneele to the Queen herself about it" — 13th October 1600 — " Your leave (of absence from Flushing) was moved by Mr Secretary, then by my Lord Admirall and then after by my Lady Warwicke. The answer her Majestie made unto them all was to one purpose: "well, well, he shall come over, but I will see further yet." My Lord Admirall besought her Majestie to let hym Know, what cawse she had to put y^t of? She answered "That he shuld not be partaker of y^t." If y^t be (said he) the advertisement your Majestie had of the Archdukes Preparacion to beseige Ostend I can assure you he hath put all his Forces into Garrison. Ostend sayd the Queen, "why may y^t not be Flushing."

25

And then I know Sidney wold not be away.' Mr Secretary (as my Lord Harbert can witness, who went this morning and spoke with his Honour, on this Matter), protestes that he did not thincke her Majestie wold have denied y^t unto hym: that he was soe farre ingaged by his Promis to you that he cold no tell what to doe to performe y^t: that he wold not give y^t over but desires others may move y^t and he will further y^t. I have gotten my Lord Treasurer (Buckhurst) to ashure me he will move y^t, to whom I have delivered all the reasons why you desire to be here. My Lady Warwicke y^s passionately troubled at y^t and cannot tell what she shuld say or thinke at her Majesties answers. Her Ladyship tells me that she cannot learne the cawse, or any cawse, why you are staied, though she pressed to Know it from my Lord Admirall and Mr Secretary, who likewise protest they doe not Know y^t." — On the 18th October (1600) Rowland Whyte goes down to Pinehurst in Kent, the seat of the Sydney family, to spend a Sunday, it being the birth day of Mistress Mary Sydney the eldest daughter of Sir Robert, to whom he writes upon the old topic. "After I had beate my Brains to find out the Mistery of your Leave not being granted I came to the Knowledge that her Majestie shuld say That she was importuned for Sidney's leave, who had no business here, but to seake a Title of Honor. Your Lordship can gather more by this then myself can conceave, for myne own Part. I see by Mr Secretaries Care, that he will use the best creditt he hath who lately said he could not make the Queen grant it, but he hoped to persuade her Majestie unto it." At last Queen Elizabeth grudgingly grants the Leave, and Whyte announces it to Sir Robert. 30th October 1600. Myne owne deere Lord — Your Leave is now graunted, but with such a due, as I never knew the like: it is minsed and sawsed, as by a Letter written unto you (which shall accompany it) from my Lord Admirall and Mr Secretary will appeare more at large. In few words, you had not come over at all, if Mr Secretary had not afsured upon his Honor that you were very ill, and that there you cold have no Remedy to prevent the Danger of your Sicknes. I was examined about it and protested, upon my Duty and allegiance to the Queen, that I understoode too well, both by your own Lettres and the report of all that came from Flushing, that you were very ill, and that it might cost you your Liffe, if this Wyenter you did not speedily take care of your Health, which cold not be done at Flushing. Mr Secretary desired the Queen to call my Lord of Rutland unto her, who lately had seen you. Her Majestie did soe and he afsured her, upon his Faith and Honour, that he left you ill, and not well able to stur out of your Chamber. These reasons induced the Queen to grant it and within 2 or 3 dayes, it will be signed & sent over unto you. I wold have had only Mr Secretaries Lettre, signifieng the Queen's Pleasure, lest it might receve a further stay, but his Honor bid me have no Feare, for now their was no cawse for it, and that her Majestie wold speedily dispatch it. Her Majestie told them, that nothing cold have moved her to have given you leave to come away from your charge but your Sickenes: but if she cold find, that it was but a Devise to amuse her, she wold take it very ill at their Hands and you shuld suffer for it, but if you were ill indeed, she then wold see that all Help shuld be ministred to prevent any further Danger, as to one she loved & cared for. My Lady Warwicke is not half well at London & when I spoke with her, last seemed to have a desperate hope of your return. My^X Lord Harbert is practicing at Greenwich, I sent him word of

---

^{X} "My Lord Harbert" (or Herbert) was the son of the Earl of Pembroke who married as his 3rd wife Mary Sydney, the sister of Sir Robert. She has been immortalised by Ben Jonson as "Sydney's sister Pembroke's mother." William, Earl of Pembroke was born in 1580 and died at

this: he leapes, he daunces, he makes his Horse runne with more Speede: he thanckes me and meanes to be exceeding merry with you this winter in Baynards Castell, where you must take Phisicke," Sir Wm Browne to Sir Robert Sydney — "Your Lordship's letter dated at Canterbury the 17th Nov^r (1600) was delivered me yesterday. I have putt Dick Smith in my mynd of your wild Boar and Rhenish Wyne & this morning I send a Drum to Sloue, who shall from my self have a Remembrance with him for Wyld Boar & when Hawkes pass by I will buy your Lordship a last of Hagard Faulcons." About this time an incident occurred at Flushing which caused the Deputy Governor some uneasinefs. He received an anonymous letter from London craftily conveying the idea that the writer (who professed to be his friend) knew he was implicated in a correspondence with the Earl of Essex & that his name was down in the bloody beadroll of those who were doomed to punishment sooner or later. Sir W^m at once wrote to Sir Robt Cecil & the Privy Council and prepared, to go over to England and demand an audience of the Queen.

Baynard's Castle the London Residence of the Sydneys. He succeeded his father in 1601, and the title passed to his brother Philip.

Ryght honorable

I am bold to wryte my generall to y[e] L[ord]: of her ma[jes]ties most ho[nora]ble privy
counsell and to finde hirein enclosed a libelling letter as 'twas yesterday
delivered to my man by an ordinary dutch post, he w[hi]ch hereby make
use herehaue if I were as very a villein as here, or at least if I were
thoght so to bee: I shold take itt as a great plague from God, if here
were any fuch enreach of mee, if itt bee butt a slaunder of a seditious
rogue, I shall account itt as a great honour to bee numbred amonge
so many most honorable and vertuous personages as here hertofore
mallice endeuourrs by scandalous libells to defame, if itt shold bee so
if fuch opinion were held of men my lyfe and goods must answere
the shame my base disloyalty to my generall I shlyne to be
knowne by all the counsell if bee a perfect honest subiect in such
respects, so do I pheartarly beseech your honor above the rest
because I honor y[ou] most, y[a]t I may bee knowne to be such
a one as is worthy to bee well accounted of: And even so
I my harty prayers to God for your honor I humbly take
leave of hisbury this 5 of July 1605 —

Your honors as much at
command as any seruant of
his

William Browne

Sir William Browne to Sir Robert Cecil Knt.

Ryght Honorable

I am bold to wryte in generall to y^r LL^s of her Mat^{ies} most hon: privy Counsell and to send herein enclosed a libelly letter wch was yesterday delivered to my man by an ordinary dutch post, he wold thereby make me beleeve y^t I were as very a villen as hee, or at least y^t I were thoght so to bee: I shold take itt as a great plague from God, if there were any such conceeyt of mee, if itt bee butt a slander of a seditious roge, I shall account itt as a great honour to bee numbered amonge so many most honorable and vertuous p'sonages as there traiterous mallice endevourets by scandelous libells to defame, if itt shold bee so y^t such opinions were held of mee, my lyfe and goods must answere wth shame my base disloyalty: as in generall I desyre to bee knowne by all the Counsell to be a p'fect honest subject in such respects, so do I p'ticularly beeseech your honor above the rest (because I honor y^w most) y^t to y^w I may bee knowne to be such a one as is worthy to be well accounted of: and even so wth my harty prayer to God for your honor I humbly take leave.

Flushing this 8th of July 1601. Your honors as much at Command as my servant y^w have   William Browne

addressed to

"To the ryght honorable Syr Robert Cecill Knight — principall Secretary to her Majesty, and master of the wards at the Court.

—To the Lords of the Privy Council —

Ryght honorable and worthy Lords —

This letter enclosed comes from one y^t termes him self my frend, butt being a scholler I learned this trew maxime y^t frendship cannot be held wth unhonest men, of wch number he appears to be by his letters, derogating in libelling sort from ye honorable and mercifull government of our Cuntry under so admirably myld and gratious a Queene. I fear I am not alone to whom he hath addrefsed desgreysed and masqued pleges of his Judas lyke meaning: His project may be to wound ye harts of poore men y^t foolishly beeleeve in him wth jealousy, discontentment, and feare where no feare is drawing them on to desperate cawses who are yett unknown and happely despayer of there owne justifications butt in Shooting at my conscience he hath lost his ayme, for I never blush when such matters are propounded and God hath given me a trew hart y^t bidds mee loose no courage. Hee seemes indeed to Know mee in part, I wold bee ashamed he shold Know me otherwyse then to bee as him selfe in a clawse of his letters confefses of mee zealous in religion, to have a loyall hart to her mat^{ie} and a dutifull affection to my country: and as for my correspondency, I ever held wth ye late Earle of Essex I call him nor none of his seditious faction to bee witnefses of my innocence, my actions shall answer for them selves whoseoever dare accuse mee: and itt is ye least part of my thought to beleeve any man y^t Shall tell mee much lefs will I beleeve such a traitour who wrytes this, y^t I am suspected wth your honors, or y^t my name is in ye bloody beadroll, as he falsly and wickedly termes itt (where so wonderfull clemency hath bene used). In ye last part of his letter wherein he layes him self too open to discovery to make mee see his dissembling villany. Hee beetwrayes also his simplicity by inserting this foolish supposition, y^t your honors would here after render other pretence send for mee: as if he, myself or any other cold bee ignorant, y^t your LL^{ps} least co mand myght bring mee over to tryall, whensoever and whersoever itt pleased yow — nolens volens. Butt I desyre no longer to live then I will runne willingly uppon the least su mons from your honours to p'forme any action co manded by yow or to justify any action I may bee accused to have done against your worthy proceedings. My conclusion is ryght honorable y^t as itt is to mee most evydent, y^t this libeller is a most lying rayler against those y^t governe the steerage of our co͞monwealth soe. I lykewise afsure myself y^t he lyes in his p'suasive speeches tending to lead in my conjecture y^t false measure were ment to my self wch I will not be so wicked as once to think. My most humble sute is to understand your LL^{ps} Comceyts of ye letters and of my self. In ye meantyme I will pray to ye allmyghty to bless all your most honorable Councells for our sovereigne Queens best service, as hitherto he hath blessed them.

From Flushing this 8th of July — 1601

This letter was delivered my man when I was att ye water gate expecting news from Ostend: at my retourne my man gave itt me in ye presence of C. Baskervyle, Capten Williams and 3 or 4 other officers. Opening itt and finding no name, reading 3 or 4 lynes in ye middle of ye letter I was astonyed and enquyred for ye bringer, he was an ordinary mefsinger of Holland. I frequently sent to seeke him, butt found him not. Before I redd further I called ye two above mentioned Captens and redd itt beefore them. I will doe my best whatsoever itt costeth to fynd out ye auctour if pofsibly I may itt was delivered mee yesterday: I wold not keep it longer then I could conveniently send itt.

I am your LL^{ps} most humble servant till death

Enclosed   William Browne

To the most honorable the Lord of her Mat^{ies} most honorable privy Counsell — give these at her Court...

— The Anonymous Letter to Sir Wm Browne —

Syr: Y^t is not unknowen to yow that a true and trusty frend is tryed in doubtful and dangerous occasions. Whereupon having alwayes harboured in my hart an unfeigned affection towardes you and yours, for yor manifold curtesyes extended to me and myne, I could not rest satisfyed in concience to have performed the part of a Kind and Constant frend, unlefs I made you partaker of such occurrences as may tend, in proceffe of tyme to the danger of yor parson, unlefse ye same be wth prudence forseene, wth discretion debated wth judgment digested and wth policye presented, and in ye discovery of this lurcking Caltroppe yow may ye more safely entreteigne a sincere conceit of myne undoubted frendship considering I doe not thereby endevour, to pike a thanck, or crave a curtesey, or clayme a requital, in as much as I conceale my name, wch of necefsity I am driven to doe especialy in these ficle tymes, in wch wheather we live in court or converse in cittye, or repose in Conntrey we find no one practice more rife and ready, then to love wyth brow and byte wyth tothe to shake wyth hand and harme wyth hart, So farfurth as that the mayster dare not trust his servant, nay the husband ye wife, ye father his sonne, ye mother her daughter, wherefore having balanced ye danger of ye tyme wyth ye favor and firmnefse of myne affection: so by the later I am moved to discover for yor securitye what I know: as by ye formour I am warned to supprefse my name in silence I much the soner, in that I stand very wel afsured, y^t yow would not wish his harme, who loveth yor good, nor covet his ruin that seketh yor saftye. Wherefor not to hold you longer in Suspense, thus standeth ye case, you are not ignorant, what doleful chang the late Earle of Essex, his sudden fal hath already made and is lyke to make here after in sundrye personages, that in calling and qualitye are honorable and worshipful, which I confefse cannot seem strange to those that are betten wyth ye mutations of worldly estates, wch undoubtedly doe leane upon such feeble brackettes that wyth ye sudden blast of an exspected Storme they are eftsoon turned upsyde downe topsyturvye: for lyke as when maine pillor falleth or sinketh, by wch a stately building is underpropt, y^t draweth downe wyth y^t a rablement of stoanes of sundrye shapes, eavenso y^t hapneth in ye ordinary course of

33

this wandring world that when great and lofty potentates fal from the top of fortune whether Sundrye others are forced to tumble down headlong wyth them to the utter overthrow of themselves and of there posteritye. how beyt their fal were the lefse to be rued, yf only ye guiltye were punished, and the faultlefse spared. But alas good Syr, the matter standeth not alwayes so sure in joynet. To omit ye tragical discourses of former ages and to cal yow home to ye view of ye present face of o^r country, wee feind therein such spiying, such paying, such shercking, such shifthing, such coyying, such foysting that many althogh otherwise true and loyal subjectes know not, whom to trust, or to what resolution to betake them selves, let a man comend ye dead, he is thereupon suspected to condemne ye quick, let hym be silent, he is heelde for particial let him converse in companye his woordes are wrested to a wrong construction. The closets and eares of o^r rulers stand always open to every promoter, his twatring tale, whomsoever they empeache is forthwyth had in jealousye. Matters are measured not by ye bright sonn beames of truth, but by ye hidden malice of lying reporters, pretending in shew her Majestyes service wurcking under hand, ye ruin of their neighbours. By wch unconscionable practifes Sundry innocent persons and sound subjects are lyke in tyme to be brought in question. In which blooddy bed rol y^{or} name (my dear frend) hath bene seene and read by a man of great calling and of no lefs credit, as himself in confident secrecye told me. I pleaded seriously for yow as reason and frendship required, by presenting before him y^{or} zeale in religion, y^{or} loyaltye to her majeistye, y^{or} dutiful affection towards y^{or} countrey & wythal, ye litle correspondencye you have had wth ye Earle of Essex, wth sundry the lyke pregnant circumstances. I wish, man, quoth he, al those poinctes I know to be as true as you can tel me: but doe you not remember Esop, his fable of ye Lyon and ye fox, that in princes courtes, some tyme a bunch of fleash is accompted an horne, and wyth this short and sharp answer he left me alone.

Wherefor good Sir, having this secret inckling given me by so great a personage, I could not suffer y^t, to burne any longer in my brest, but holde y^t for Convenient to acquaynt yow wth ye contentes of ye co͞munication, that hereby yow may prevent ye malitious packing of yor secret foes, according to ye old sayd saw — Once warned, haulf armed. —

Thus have I layed open this festring sore, wishing y^t lay in my power to find owt som fit salve that might heale y^t, but y^t I refer to yor good consideration. Howbeyt I am of opinion, that y^t will not be amisse to dissemble ye matter for none would confefse y^t albeyt he were Charged therewyth, and wth I suppose y^t ye lords of ye Counsayl wil not acquaynt yow wth ye form o^r surmises, as long as yow live in ye place and charge yow possesse, but rather they wyl devise how to trayne yow from thence, when ye heat of these present garboyles shal be somewhat afswaged, by pretending some colourable conference wth yow, concerning such poynctes, as appertaine to yor charge. The Lord so direct yow in al yor proceedinges, send yow of his grace in as ample wise as I wish to myne owne soule.

ffrom my lodging in london the 15th of June 1601.

Yo^r most afsured

N.L.

Sir I kept this letter, this moneth and more Expecting to hit upon som trusty frend, and so having found a marchant bound for ffrance, I requested him to endorse the letter in ye ffrench ton.

Thus endorsed in a french hand

A monsieur

Monsr Guillaume Browne, Lieutenant gouverneur della ville

de flisinge, a flisinge —

Sir William Browne to Sir Robert Sydney.

My most honorable good Lord

On Saturday last in the Morning, I delivered your Lordship's Letters to Mr Secretary: he was pleased to lett the Queenes Letters be delivered by my self: and very honorably on Sunday Morning after Prayers, the Queen walking into the Gardens at Sir William Clarks, after, Mr Bodeley had first spoken 4 or 5 Words with her Majestie, Mr Secretary mentioned me: she presently called for mee, and was pleased to say I was welcomm, with many good Wordes. I must tell your Lordship, that before, having had no Conference with Mr Secretary about any Busines, he had told me in the Morning, in pafsing from his Coach into the Court, that he had informed the Queen how much I was grieved according to that your Lordship had written unto him, and told me, that her Majestie wold speake with mee, and that then I knew well enough how to answer her: and so, in deed, I had no sooner Kyfsed her sacred Hands, butt that she presently made me stand upp, and spoke somewhat lowd, and sayd, Com hether Browne: and pronounced that she held me for an old faithful Servant of hers, and said, I must give Content to Browne, or som such Speeches: and then the Trayne following her, she sayd, Stand, stand back, will you not let us speake, but you wilbe Hearers? And then walked a Turne or two protesting her most gracious Opinion of my self: And before God, Browne, sayd shee, they do me Wrong that will make so honest a Servant be jealous that I should mistrust him. I forgott to tell your Lordship, that when I first Kneeled, I delivered your Lordships Letter, which she received, butt redd itt not till I was gone from her. I told her Majestie that your Honour did not tell itt me in any such Sort, butt that I being your Officer, to whom, in your Absence, you used to leave the Charg of her Majesties cautionary Towne, you cold, for your owne Afsurance, do no lefs but seeke Meanes to be most afsured of me and mine: whereuppon she Told me, in what Order she had spoken to your Lordship, much to that Purpose itt pleased you to tell me: and told me of that of my Lady Morgan: but added, that she had that afsurance of me to, and thoghe her word alone had bene more than sufficient to content so mean a Servant of my self, yett itt pleased her to swear unto me, That she had as good affiance in my loiolty, as in any Man that served her. My Answers your Lordship may gefse at, and my Joy then hath made me joyful ever since: But I must not forget to tell your Lordship, that having walked a Turne or twoo, she called for a Stoole, which was sett under a Tree, and I began to Kneele, butt she wold not suffer mee: in so much as that after twoo or three Denyalls which I made to Kneele, still she was pleased to say, that shee wold not speake with mee unles I stood upp. Whereuppon I stood upp and after having reconfirmed her royall favour, and gracious Opinion of me. she discoursed of many Things, and particularly of the Distast she had of the States Armyes retourning: and it seemes, to your Lordship be it spoken, that Sir Fr. Vere hath layn all the Fault uppon Conte Maurice: yett I answered thus much, that I hard that Counte Maurice did protest, that this Journey was never of his Plotting, nor much allowed of by him: Tush, Browne, saith she, I know more then thou doest: When I hard said shee, that they were, at the first, with there Army as hygh as Nemegham, I knew then that no Good wold be done, butt Maurice to serve his owne Turne wold, in the Ende, turne to the Grave: I looked they shold have comm downe nearer to Ostend, or have taken som Towne in the Hart of Brabant, or Flanders, that myght have startled the Enemy: and that they promysed mee: or els I wold not have lett them have so many Men: and with much Discontent to my Subjects, as I know, butt for the love which they bear mee they would not so well digest, and now, forsooth, Morrice is comme from his Weapon to the Spade, for att that he is one of the best in Christendom. Itt was not beefitting for mee to answer any Thing for him, when I saw her Majestie so informed alredy: the Truth must appear to her in Tyme, and from a better Hand then my self. Then she talked of the French King, what he had promysed them: I answered, that we receaved itt as Certen, that the French King rather marvelled att there foolish Boldnes in venturing there Army so farr, then that he ever gave them any Afsurance to joyne with them. Tush, Browne, sayd shee, do not I know that Bucenvall was written to, and written too again, to move the Army to go that Way, and that then he wold help them? If that were so, sayd I, then your Majestie may thinke itt was butt a French Promys. I can not think of all the Discourses we hadd, yett the one Thing I must not forgett to tell your Lordship, that I told her, the Hope of those of Zeland, consisted alone in her Majestie, by whose commanding Motion to the States Generall there Army myght be brought to do somewhat of Moment in those Parts. Alas! poore Zelanders, said her Majestie I know that they love me with all there Harts. I added, that they prayed continually for her: Yea, Browne, sayd shee, I know itt well enoughe: and I wlll tell thee one thinge: Faith, here is a Church of that Cuntrymen in London, I protest, next after the divine Provydence that governs all my well doing, I attribute much of the Happiness which befalls mee, to be given me of God by those mens effectuall and zealous Prayer, who I Know pray with that Fervency for me, as none of my Subjects can do more. After long Talk, at length Mr Secretary Came, who was pleased to grace me still more and more, and Talk was ministred again of the Army: Mr Secretary sayd, that if it pleased her Majestie, itt were not amyfs if Mr Vere were writt to, for to procure that his Part of the Army myght be drawne downwards towards Ostende. Her Majestie presently sayde unto mee Dost thou see that little Fellow that Kneels there: itt hath bene told you that he hath bene an Enemy to Souldiours: on my Faith Browne, he is the best Frend the Souldiours have. He answered, That itt was from her Majestie alone, from whom flowed all Souldiours Good. The Ende was, wherwith I will end my Letter, that I received perfect Joy by being so favoured of her Majestie, as that I shall think of itt during Lyfe, and will never bee forgetfull to bee most humbly loving to you, from whom the Begining and the Continuing of my wellfare, proceedeth: which harty Confefsion of myne, I hope, is Acknowledgment sufficient, till my Deedes may bear Witnes to my Wordes. I leave all the Newes, which is very small, to be discoursed of by Mr White, whose Letter your Lordship shall receive herewith. On Saturday I will wryte again if any Thing fall out, in the mean Tyme, worthy your Knowledg. From London this 12th of August, 1601.

Your Honor &c &c

William Bowne.

Postscript — "My Lord, I send you with this Letter all the Queen's Entertainment at Cheswicke and att my Lord Keepers, I have gotten them coppyed out for you. We dranke, yesternyght, a Health to your Lordship, at my Lord of Pembrooke, where was Sir Henry Leonard, my Lady Ann mends very well." Sir William was in England early in July 1602 and writes to Sir Robert that he "arrived at Margett and the next morning took horse towards London, stayed 2 Howers att Canterbury where in your Lordshipps name, I saluted Mr Manwood and of him borrowed a Gelding whereon I sett Lieut Johnson and from Sittingbourne sent him the next day to Penshurst, myself came the same day to London and about 6 of the clock, very weary, yett made a stopp to my lord of Pembrooke, whom I found not within. my lady Anne kept her chamber. There I mett with Sir

39

Henry Leonard whose good company stayed me there so long, till my Lord himselfe came in, to whom I delivered your Lordship^s letter and so toke Leave, because thoghe it was 8 of the clock yett I wold trye where to gett Horses to go in the morning to the Court, where I hope to bee beefore they bee removed: for as, I hear, itt laye yesterdaye at Sir William Clasken butt is this day to remove somewhat nearer Otelands where it is thought it will stay 8 or 10 dayes and althogh that her Majesty hath sent my Lord of Hertford word, that yet she meanes to see him notwithstanding itt is held the determined Progress is at the furthest. xxxx I am now putting Foot in Sturrop this present Saturday morning at 4 of the clock the 7th of July 1602.

I am and always wil be your Lordships &c Wm Browne

My most honored good Lord - - - - Since my coming into Engl^d I have only received one Letter from your Lordship. I have bene in the Country and am retourned and now will, upon your Lordships summons retourn to Flushing, butt wold humbly desyre your Lordship for my safe coming that your Lordship wil be pleased that Sometymes that the next week a man of Warr, may be procured to com on this Coast, to take mee in, least I miss of other convoy: uppon Knowledg that he is com either to Dover Sound, or Margett I wil be with him in 24 Houres, God willing. On Friday or Saturday I go to court, where I wilbe 4 or 5 dayes & then Know, if any Service will be comanded me of your Lordship and if I receive any letters for your Lordship, will presently dispatch one with the letters, though myself perhapps shall staye 4 or 5 Dayes after, uppon private businef. The Serjant Major's man came hither on Monday last and went the same day to the Court: itt seemes that he brought the newes of Master Gilpin's Death, for whose Place I hear there are many Sutors, and if I thoght I myght prevayle, I wold speak for my selfe. The Serjant Major wrytes unto mee that certain English Prisoners at Sluce rayle

40

bitterly and speake vilanously of mee: butt what they say particularly, he wrytes not: itt is my Ponishment to be payd with Ingratitude where I have well deserved, for I protest before God, I have laboured all the Wayes possible I cold, to doo them good. London September the 15th 1602.

The George Gilpin, alluded to in the above letter, had been the Secretary to the Embassy to the States General at the Hague for several years.

Sir William returns to Flushing, and writes to Sir Robert 16 of October 1602, that he arrived there on the Tuesday morning after his departure, "and sooner he cold not have we retourned." xxxx "when I came to the Haghe the Greffin Aerssens and divers others, and many of our nation, were of Opinion, that I came to be in Gilpin's place, butt I told your lordship what Blocks were in my way neither indeed do I desyre itt (seing Mr Edmonds, my deare Frend and one that honours your Lordship is lyke to have itt, in case Mr Bodely refuse itt) but this I humbly desyre your Lordship to do for me, that you will testify to Mr Secretary that I did not idly desire it without having some sufficiency, to do her Majesty service in the Place." — Flushing 29th November 1602. " His Excellency pretends to the Tenth part of the Carrack and I think shall have itt and the States of the Land the 5th. I have bought a Turkey Carpet for my Lord of Bergeveny, 7 Dutch Ells long, itt cost 27 £ Sterling butt it is estemed very fine & well worth the money. Whyte Quilts of Calico, stitcht with Silk are 7 £ & 8 £ Sterling the peece: in fine there is nothing almost that is good, cheap, but Trash: at Flushing your Lordship's Government, all Things are well, God be thancked and the Plague diminisheth: Mr Danyell began yesterday again to preach in our Church. All the English Captens have there Commissions directly from the States and are sworn to them. I hear that of late Sir Francis Vere, ryding abroad in his Coach, mett his Excellencys coach and pafsed by with out saluting him: and that afterwards he sent his Excuse, saying that he was sorry and that he sawe not his Excellency's coach because itt passed uppon his blynd Syde: I hear that his Excellencys answer was, that itt was a blynd Excuse."

Reports reach Holland that Queen Elizabeth is very ill and the Hollanders express much concern, a boat from Gravesend arrives and its passengers are questioned and assure them that "Her Majesty had been somewhat sick but not any way in Daunger of Death. I caused presently this newes to be sent them: it was so pleasing to this Towne, as on my Faith your Lordship might see sodain Chaunge, in there Faces for Joye and myself Captain Fleming, Captain Ray, the Burgomaster and 6 or 7 more of the best Sort went and drunke good Carrowses in Renyshe wyne to her Majesties Health. (22nd March 1602.)

Three days after, the following letter was received, of the Queen's death, when King James 1st was proclaimed with great ceremony, by Sir William Brown at Flushing & Sir Francis Vere at Brille.

Sir William Browne to Sir Robert Sydney on the death of Queen Elizabeth

My most honorable good Lord.

I received your Lordships, dated the 25th of March by Mr Cuntstable, the 29th of the same: the contents of your Letters Certefying the Death of our late dread Soverign, and the proclayming of our ryghtfull Kinge, Kinge James, bredd in many Hartes mingled Passions, Sorrow for the Lofse of one, under whose Gouverment we had so long lived happy: and Gladnes, that God, in his mercifull Provydence, had so disposed of the Succefsion to the Crowne, as that both the Ryght of Succeeding was held inviolate, and he, who by that Ryght is proclaimed respected, and undowtedly esteemed of all Men, that have been trewly informed of his Vertues, a most worthy, and that so Excellent Prince

42

from whom we can expect, by his good and godly Government, rather an augmentinge, then diminishing of our forepassed Happiness. uppon the Receipt of your Lordship's Letter, I foreslowed no Tyme to proclaime him in this Garrison accordingly, as your Letter had instructed me: but first I sent for the Burghomasters and Secretary and Jacques Gelley (Ja. Fransen was sick) Luvesson, with the Secretary and Gelley came: I delivered them your Lordship's Desyre, and after gave them your Letter: they made Shew to be very willinge to doo what was befitting: I told them, that the same Day, by 12 of the Clock, I would assemble the Souldiours and procalayme him, and wished them to be ready to accompany me at the same Tyme: it was uppon Tuesday, our Market Day: This I delivered them in the Morninge, and presently dispatched my Servant with Letters to Mr Valck, desyringe him to Communicate to the States my Intention, following the Proceeding in England, to publish the Proclamation in Flushing, wishing them to depute som, if they thoght it fit, to accompany me in the Doing of it. Our Burgomaster, presently after our Conference, assembled in the Stathouse, and upon Consultation Luvefson and the Secretary went them selves to the States, at Middlebourgh to conferre with them: in the mean Time, I commanded all our Souldiours to be in armes at there Ensines Lodginge, that at an instant upon my Summons, they might come into the Market Place. It was longe before the Burgomaster retourned from Middlebourgh, neither hard I any Thinge from thence, till it was neare 12 of the Clock, at length my Man and they came almost together, and sent me Word, that the States themselves were lykewyse up on the Way: whereuppon myself, with the Serjeant Major, went, in the mean Tyme, to the Statehowse, where I spoke again to the Burgomasters, and some of the Counsell: but whyle I was on this Conference, about there joyning with me, Word was broght that the States were come: only that Mr Valck comming by Skute was not yet arryved: I broke of my Speech thereuppon, because they seemed willing that I shold communicate it with the States: Valck arryved not long after, and then the States sent unto me a Messenger to tell me, that they were come expressly to conferre with me & that if, in the After Noone, I wold be at Leysure, they wold come Home unto me. I sent one expressly unto them, to desyre them, that, for all Matter of Importance, they wold come unto the Stathowse presently, which they did: There, after other Preface which I thoght fit, I told them what I had moved, and what I found reasonable the Burghers of the Towne shold do in this Busines, and used such arguments, as my poore Wit cold best frame: Vanderwerck, in the Name of the rest (for it seemed they had before imagined what I wold demaunde) begonne his Answer, with a Protestation of the Grief generally conceaved for the Losse of so worthy a Queen, to whose Goodnes there whole Country was so much, and so infinitly bound: but seing that every ones Dayes were in the Hands of the Lord, they cold not but content them selves with his good Will and Pleasure: and that in this Affliction, it was no small Comfort unto them, to hear how peaceably Things were determined of in England, for the Establishment of the Succession uppon the King of Skotland and whom they had ever bene in good Favour and League with all, and from whom they expected, and hoped all wyse lovinge, and carefull Consideration of there Estates: and to that Ende to shew with what Gladnes they received the Newes of his beinge proclaymed in England, they were all of them, as many as were at Home come to congratulate with me for it: but that I knew, that they being but a Member of the whole Body, cold not determine of any Thing, without advysing with the other Provinces: that they made no Question but that, uppon general Consultation, Contentment shold be given as was requysite: and that, in the meane Tyme, they did with all Gladnes give Applause to the Proclayminge. My

Answer, as the Sodain gave me Leave to judge fit, was, that thoghe I cold wish they all joyned, yett that seinge itt cold not stand with there united Correspondence, that I wold not move them of Zeland in generall unto itt, butt that I cold do no lefse for the afsurance of our mutuall Affections in this Town: seing that we did take the Oath of Obediance to the Kinge, and maintayninge of the Contracts, that the Burghers shold lykewyse doo the lyke, till further Agreement were concluded betweene the King's majesty and the States Generall, and that this was fitt for the government: or else we shold dout with what Autority to commaund, and they not be resolute in their Devotion to obey, as was meet for the safe Keeping of this Towne: the Serjeant Major was present all this Tyme. Having thus ended, telling them how acceptable such forwardness wold be, I ryse upp & went out, & gave them leave to deliberate: the Burghomasters, after having had some Conference with them, went asyde lykewyse into another Chamber by themselves. I was not longe after sent for in again, & then Vanderwerck for the rest sayd, that they afsured themselves, that I did understand well there Country Government, & that for them at Flushing to take a new Oath, without Consent of the rest, were to severe them from the other Townes: and that there was no occasion for me to dout of all good Correspondence: for that they did not understand that any Man was by the Death of the Queene discharged of their Oath for observing the Contract: and desyred that for a whyle I wold be contented with that Satisfaction. My Answer was, that they shold perceive by my Proceeding that I wold urge them no Way further then Reason requyred, and therefore wold frame my Request according to their own Discourse, that seeing they cold not approve that as yett a new Oathe shold be offered to the Burghers in Flushing: yet that itt myght by Proclamation be made Knowne by the Burghomasters to all the Inhabitants, that there Oathe heretofore made for holdinge & mainteyning the Contract between

45

the Queen's majesty, of famous memory and them, was still remayning in full Force, Strength and Virtue, whereof they were all to take Knowledge, that itt might in all Respects be observed. This they cold not say much against: and so in the Ende itt was concluded, which was all I cold do for the present, which I hope, your Honour will hold sufficient, seing our Command is after a sort (more precario): After this, being allmost 2 of the clock, I proceaded to the Proclamation, which, by good Fortune, Mr Cuntstable had broght over with him, myself redd itt in the Statehouse Bay window, being accompanyed by the States of Zeland, as many as were att Home, and not Sick: Malrey was sick: there were present Valck, Huessens, Vanderwerck, Myrons, Oleartsen, Zuytland and Bonifacius: these all leaned out att the Wyndowes by mee, as lykewyse did the Burghomasters, and som of the best Burghers, and the preachers of the Towne in an other Chamber, so that itt was done with great Solemnity, and acclamation of all Sortes: when the printed Proclamation was redd out, I then followed the Contents of your Lordships Letter, that concurring with what was done in Englande, by authority and Command: From the Lord Governor being absent, I Liefftenant Governor, Serjeant Majour, Captens &c &c of this Garrison were to take our Oath of Allegiance for defending and mainteyninge of this Towne, with hazard of Lyfe and Goodes, to the Behoof of our Kings Ryght, following the Contract &c, till further Order were to be established. This I red Word by Word out of Your Lordship's Letter, only adding for the Burghers better Contentment, till further Order were established. At the Ende of all, I Commanded the Souldiours, in Syne of there Loyalty and joyfull receiving the Oath, to hold up their Hand, and say, God Save Kinge James: which they all did: and after to conclude, delivered two very excellent Vollys of Shott and were answered by the Ordinance rounde about the wall. When this was finished, having more Devotion to eat, having fasted all Day, than to hear a Sermon, we went presently to the Landryght, where my self, the Serjeant Major, and the rest of the Captains, had determyned on our owne Purses to have been merry with the Burghomasters: butt the States Coming also, the Burghomaster defrayed all: and we were drunke all in drinking the Health of our King: To end my Letter, let me afsure your Lordship, that never any Governour had more firmely affectionate Hartes to his Service then your Lordship hath in this Garrison: and for my own Particular I will never be otherwyse. At nyght we shott of our Ordinance doble again round about the Wall, and made Fires of Joy: God send our King James long Lyfe. Flushing, this 4th of Aprill — 1603.

your Lordships &c

William Browne

Sir William Browne to Lord Sydney (created in 1603)

"I have received your Honours Letter, dated the 18th of February. I acknowledg your Honours especiall Love towards me, in that itt pleaseth you to make me know how matters stand between the Lord Cecill and yourself: my comfort is that he shall not find any Staff to beat a Sydney and good my Lord (thogh I be not worthy to counsell you) yet give me leave to deliver my advyse: that in no case (seing your Honour is innocent of any just Imputation of wronging him) you make semblant to care what he unjustly conceyves of you, for so undowtedly he will sooner be broght to fynd his own Errour thereby any Protestation that he were misinformed. Perhaps he is lyk som Women, who seekes them that sue not unto them, and flye from those that adore them. If my Hart were not fixed in trew Duty and Love I am bound to respect your Honour, or I wold never wryte thus boldly and plainly butt beccaus I love zealously I can not hold my Peace, yett cold I wish that all were at Peace with you, so itt may be done without Impeachment to your Honour. I will add hereunto a little secret Fear which I, by much adoe, did somewhat wringe out of Malrey: he spake of Sir Anthony Standen's Errors, & of his Commissions received and that he was especially directed to the Queen's Majesty as in afsurance of her religion and that she shold persuade the King to chaunge his religion: and he added that if all were trew which he had hard in secret that there were many great Ones in England that were not Frends to the Religion. I answered what I thoght fitt and drew my arguments from the Ladyes that her Majesty pleased to use as Companions, assuring him, that they were all of the reformed religion. He seemed to tell itt mee in great Secrett as thoghe he were Loath I shold speak of it to your Honour. I wryte itt that you may lett me have notice if itt were so and what hopes I may boldly give to the contrary. Flushing 26th February — 1603.

Sir Horatio Vere to Sir William Browne

Good Father. . . . I thanke you very mutch for the Letters you sent me: if y^t falls within the Cumpasse of my Power to doe you anie acceptable service you shall fynde me redie: you have the maine of your honest Frends, of Flushinge emongst us, that I do forbeare to acquaint you with our occurances. In the last Busyness we had to do, with the Enimis, Capt Williams behaved himself very worthilie with the Troope he commaunded. We mist a fayre occasion to have done a good Dayes Worke, which, I doubt not, but you have hard y^t at large. So with my Kindest Salutations and my Prayers for your Health, I recommend you to the Almighty Protection and rest your lovinge Son and most assured Frend to be commanded.

Campe the 21st of May — 1604.   — H. Vere —

Arthur Collins says in a note that "this Sir Horatio Vere was the youngest son of Geoffrey Vere of Kirby Hall in Essex, 3rd and youngest son of John Earl of Oxford, who died at his manor of Colne Essex on 21st March. 31. Henry VIII. Sir Horatio was knighted for his valour at the taking of Cadiz 1596 and before that time had signalized himself in the wars of the Low Countries. Both he & his brother Sir Francis in their Letters to Sir Wm Browne subscribe themselves, your loving son, whereby it may be presumed they were initiated by him in the Military Art, for I don't find they were any way allied. In the year 1600 he with his brother Sir Francis gained great renown in the Battle of Newport and shewed, none were then equal to the English in courage or conduct. In 44. Elizth Sir Francis Vere was appointed General of all the Dutch Forces without and within Ostend with an absolute authority and commission. Horatio was made Lord Vere of Tilbury by King James — 25 July in the 1st year of his reign. The two brothers were buried near each other in Westminster Abbey.

Capt Williams to Sir William Browne

Extract — "Your letter came in Tyme, ells I would have bene so bould as to have chiden you for forgetting your poor Frend: however the common oppinion is that Red bearded men are unfaythfull yet I have never found any more honest and that yow shall always find in me and if I prove otherwise to you, I will willingly be accompted a vilayin." &c. From the Army 22 May 1604.

Sir William Browne to Lord Sydney (on the peace with Spain)

Ryght honorable my most honored good Lorde.

Itt pleased your Honour to give me Leave to wryte of the State of this Towne, becaus the necessity of providing for itt myght be urged as well by others as yourself: I have therefore written unto the Lords of the Councell for my discharge and for your service and I hope your Honour, will allow of itt; I send herein a coppy of what I have written both to them and to my Lord Cecill in private. Your Honour is still expected hear and questionles your Presence myght Confirme many affections that are already weak in these Partes through the Peace, whom I do what I can to comfort. As yett we live in all Love together, butt I feare this new cloth of Peace putt in our old Clothing of Correspondence will in Tyme teare the garment in Sunder. For my Part, I hope in your Honours absence to performe the part of an honest man and will wear my self out beefore I be weary to do your service and if your Honours private occasions keep you from coming over I humbly desyre that you will continually send me your advyse how to carry myselfe & what secrett comfort I may give either the State in Generall or there Townsmen in particular. I can wryte no newes butt that the States Generall are still dayly Expected: the Princess hath bene at Sluce and there is still and Seekes, as I understand, to plant her son in the Command of these partes. Flushing 24. August 1604.

Sir William Browne to Robt Lord Sydney

"I can send you no newes by this Bearer, more than that the States General are howerly expected. Having understood by your Honours Letter that you are busy about the marriage of your Eldest daughter, I with the rest of your Captens, have given Order to Mr Meredith to present 200 £ in our Names to buy her a chayne of Perles, or otherwise to employ as she pleases. We humbly desyre that it may be accepted as a Remembrance of the Love of her poore Servants hear. We will all pray for her Happines in the Choice and for your and my Ladyes Hartes content: and so with rememberance of my most humble services, I committ your Honour to the Allmighty. Vlushinge this 25. August - 1604.

Mary the oldest daughter of Lord Sydney was married 27 Sep^t 1604 to Sir Robert Wroth of Durants in Endfield Middlesex and of

Loughton hall Essex. They were the ancestors of the Earls of Rochford. The News of the Gunpowder Plot arrives at Flushing and Sir William writes to Lord Viscount Lisle (newly created) that "the States have on Wednesday next proclaymed a solemne Day of Fast and Prayer and that only for a Thanksgiving to God, for the Kings late miraculous deliverance: the which they confess, did concerne nearly, not only themselves but also the Prosperity of all the reformed religion throghe all Christendem. Seing the Earle of Northumberland hath so vilainously and devishly forgot himself, I am sory that ever I honored him and more sory that I have a Chyld that carryes his name. Now that Sir Franceys Vere is comm to Bril (for by som who came from Gravesend I hear that he embarqued 2 dayes agoe) we shall understand shortly how the States and he will agree. Malrey told me yesterday that he heares Mr Winwood will give over his Place and hath already written about it to my Lorde of Salisbury. Flushing 2nd November 1605.

Sir William Browne to Robert Lord Viscount Lisle

"On Saturday last we heard by great Chaunce the newes how wonderfully God hath lately preserved his Majesty, the Queen Prince, and all his Nobility and Commons. A gentleman coming from Gravesend gave me the Proclamation for the taking of Percy which confirmed the Newes to be afsuredly true. I sent the sayd Proclamation on Sunday Morning to M. Malrey — the Straungnes of the Conspiracy, was wonderfully admyred, but the goodnes of God's miraculous deliverance was more mervailled at. The same day publiq Thanks were give to God, both in Dutch and English Churches and by order from the States we triumphed for itt the same nyght, and the night following they did the like at Sluce and Isendick. I send your Honour enclosed a letter this day received from the Zeland admirall who is at this Instant in Holland. The passage is now going away so that I have but Leisure to say that I am

51

your Honours &c   Wm Browne Flushing this 13 Nov[r] 1605.

This allusion above, to the naming of his son Percy, after Henry, 9th Earl of Northumberland, refers to a friendship contracted with that Nobleman, by Sir W[m] Browne, when they served together in 1585, under Rob[t] Dudley Earl of Leicester in Holland. Thomas Percy (a Catholic) who was one of the conspirators of the Gunpowder Plot, was the cousin of the Earl of Northumberland and agent on his Estates. It was for his capture that the Proclamation in Holland was issued. He was wounded at his capture in England & died of his injuries. On the barest suspicion that the Earl of Northumberland had some knowledge of the Plot, he was thrown into the Tower, fined 30.000 £, and kept 15 years in confinement. This horribly unjust sentence was no doubt due to the jealousy and malice of Cecil who had worked upon the timid nature of James. Anthony Wood speaks in the highest terms of the Earls character, and Sir Wm Browne in honouring him with his confidence and esteem showed great judgment and discrimination, and it is much to be regretted that he did not live long enough to see the Earls character triumphantly cleared.

Sir Wm Browne to Robert Lord Viscount Lisle

"My Lord of Cramburne (the son of Cecil) had been this passage in England if he had not received contrary advyse from my Lord his father. He stayed but one day at the Haghe and one night he stayed at Middleburgh and this day he came to Flushing, where he was entertayned as well by our Garrison, as our Possibilites cold afford: and his Lordship was pleased to take a poore Dinner at my Howse, but thogh I offered it him, he wold in no case accept of Lodging in my Howse. He thinks to go this Nyght, or rather at 3 of the clock, in the morning, to embarque himself in his Excellencies yacht to go to anwerp and to see the Archdukes Countreyes in his Retourne homewardes. This is all I will now say, but that the States have consented both to the King of

Denmarck and the King of Sweden, to provide themselves of Mariners in these Partes. His Excellency will be in Zeland about the Middle of Aprill if he can recover his Health. God keep your Honour and all yours. Vlushing this 12th of march 1610   Your Honours &c William Browne.

This letter terminates the Browne Correspondence, edited by Arthur Collins in 1746. Many more remain among the family papers at Penshurst Kent, now in the possession of Lord de L'Isle and Dudley, the lineal representative of Sir Robt Sydney. In the 3rd Report of the Royal Commifsioners on Historical MSS in 1872 it is stated there are at Penshurst "26 volumes of letters of which 6 are lettered on the back as having been published by Collins. These 6 are not mentioned in the following brief list. Vol. 1. This folio, contains letters in French Latin & English. Some few from & to Sir Wm Browne, 2 letters by Mr de Blocq to Sir William Browne. – Vol 3. Thomas Ogle to Sir William Browne dated from the camp near Beile. 10. July. Sir Wm Browne (at Flushing) to Sir Robert Sydney in London (many). Letters and draughts of letters by the same to the same. Vol VI (1601-4) 1604 — Letters by Sir Wm Browne at Flushing to Lord Sydney, Lord Chamberlain to the Queen and Governor of Flushing, at the court or at Baynard's Castle. Vol VII. Labelled 1605-1606. A thick volume containing letters by Sir William Browne at Flushing, J Throckmorton & others. and a few by John Throckmorton and others. Vol VII. A thick volume containing letters by Sr Wm Browne and a few by John Throckmorton and others. Vol IX — Labelled 1610 - 1612. A thick volume containing Letters by Sir Wm Browne to Lord Sydney down to August - 1610." —

Extract from a letter to the Earl of Shrewsbury (one of the Privy Council) from Sir William Brown

"I send your Lordship here inclosed some verses compounded

by Mr Secretary who gott Hales to frame a ditty unto itt. The occasion was as I hear, y^t the young Lady of Darby wearing about her neck, in her bosom, picture which was in a dainty tablet, the Queen, espying itt, asked what fyne jewell that was: The Lady Darby was curious to Excuse the Shewing of itt, butt the Queen wold have itt and opening itt, and fynding itt to be Mr Secretaryes, snatcht itt away and tyed itt uppon her shoe and walked long with itt there: then she tooke itt thence and pinned itt on her elbow and wore itt somtyme there also: which Mr Secretary being told of, made these verses and had Hales to sing them in her Chamber. Itt was told her Majesty y^t Mr Secretary had rare musick and songs: She would needes hear them and so this ditty was soung which you see first written. More verses there be lykewise, whereof som or all, were lykewyse soung. I do boldly send these things to your Lordship wch I wold not do to any els, for I heare they are very secrett. Some of the verses argew that he repynes not thoghe her Majesty please to grace others and contents himselfe with the favours he hath. I am now in hast butt will wryte again when I have bene at Court: in the meane tyme will pray for your Lordship and my most honorable lady and remayne ever &c

18 September 1602   William Browne

Note. Sir William also wrote other letters to the Earl of Shrewsbury — from Fulham 17 September 1602 — from London 21st September 1602 and from Snelston his country seat the 9th October 1609.

Will of Sir William Brown Knight.

In the name of God, Amen, I, Sir William Browne of Snelston in the Countie of Derbye, Knight, beying whole of body and perfect of memorye considering with myselfe the mortalitye and uncerteyntie of humane life and purposing to dispose and set downe in what manner my

54

Landes and Tenements hereafter mentioned as shall be and remayne after my deathe to the pleasure of Almighty God, I do therof make this my last will & testament in wryting in manner folowing that is to saye Whereas I am seised in ffee simple of and in three messuages — fortie acres of Land, twentie acres of meadowe, one hundred acres of pasture and twentie acres of wood with the appurt'nces in Snelston, Roston, Norbury, Publye, Clifton, Edlaston and Alvaston in every or any of them, set lying or beying in the Countie of Staffordshire and allso of and in six messuages — One hundred acres of Land, fortie acres of meadow, three hundred acres of pasture and forty acres of wood with the app'tnces in Snelston, Roston, Norbury, Cubley, Clifton, Edlaston and Alvaston, or in every or any of them in the Countie of Derbie of and in which premises I stand and am seized of an estate of Inheritance in ffee simple as afore sayed and hould the same by Sucadge Tenure by vertue of Twoe severall Recoveryes thereof respectively, suffred by me with voucher over of the common vouchers uppon twoe severall writts of Entrie broughte against me by the name of William Browne, gentleman, by William Gray of Shirley, in the said Countie of Derbye, Esquire and Philipp Harison of London gentleman, (as by the said severall Recoveryes and the Records thereof in the Courte of Common pleas in the tearme of Sr Hillarye in the fower and thirtieth yere of the Raigne of our Soveraigne Ladye Elizabeth the Queenes most excellent majestie, that nowe is and by one deede declaring the uses thereof bearing date the Eighteenth daye of March in the fower and thirtieth yere of the raigne of the said soveraigne Lady the Queene amongst other thinges more at large may appeare. All which Mefsuages, Landes, Tenements and hereditaments above specified in every of the said severall Counties of Staffordshire and Derby I do give and bequeath unto Mary my lovinge wife, To have and to hould all and single the premises with the app'tnces unto my said wife for and during

55

her naturall life for her better mayntennance and for and towardes the vertuous Education of my children and after her descease I do devise & bequeath all and singular the Remaynder and Remaynders, Reverstion and Revertions of all and singular the premises with the app'tnces unto my trustie and well beloved officers, Sir Wm Russell, Kn^t, Sir Robt Sydney Kn^t, Peter Manwood in the Countie of Kent, Esquire, Thomas Edmonds Esquire Clerk of the Councell, Rowland White and Philip Harison Gentlemen and to their heires, neverthelefse uppon confidence and truste reposed by me in them and every of them and in the heires of the Survivour of them that within convenient tyme after my deathe at the costs and chardges of my said wife (if she shall then be living) and yf she shall be dead then with the yssues and profitts of my said Mefsuages, Landes, Tenements and Heriditaments above mentioned that the said Sir William Russell, Sir Robt Sidney Kn^t, Peter Manwood Esqr Thomas Edmonds Esqr Rowland White and Philip Harison Gents and the survivor of them or the heires of the survivor of them shall cause and procure all such my children which have been borne out of the Realme and here after shall be borne out of the Realme and which shall then be living to be made free denizens and capable to purchase use & enjoye Landes, Tenements and within the Realme by suche good wayes and meanes so shall be avayleable and sufficient in the Lawe and after such denizations so had and procured I will and my Intent and Mynde is that the sayd Sir Wm Russell Kn^t, Sir Robt Sydney, Peter Manwood Thomas Edmonds, Rowland White and Philipp Harison and the survivor of them and the heires of the survivor of them according to my truste and confidence in them and every of them by me reposed as is aforesaied shall within convenient tyme sufficientlie in the Lawe conveye and afsure all and singular the said messuages, Lands, Tenements and Hereditaments with the app'tnces unto suche of my children as shall then be myne oldest

56

sonne and then beying a denizen, to have & to houlde the same unto hym and to the heires males of his bodye and for default of suche yssue the Remaynder of all and singular as the premises with the appurtenances unto such as shall be my second sonne and then beying allso a denizen and to the heires males of his bodye lawfullie begotten — and for defaulte of such yssue the Remaynder of all and singular the premises with the app'tnces unto such as shall then be my third sonne and then living allso a denzen and to the heires males of his bodye lawfullie begotten — and for defaulte of such yssue the Remaynder of all and singular premises with the app'tnces unto such as shall then be my fourth sonne beyng then allso a denizen and to the heires males of his bodye lawfullie to be begotten and for defaulte of such yssue or yf I shall have no sonne living nor any yssues male of their bodyes — Then my will and intent is that the said Sir William Russell, Sir Robt Sydney, Peter Manwood, Thos Edmonds, Rowland White and Philipp Harison and the survivor of them and the heires of the Survivors of them shall within convenient tyme after my deathe as aforesayd sufficiently afsure and convey all and singular the said Mefsuages, Landes, Tenements, hereditaments, and all and singular the premises with the app'tnces to all and every of my daughters, which then shall be living and denizens and to the heires of their severall bodyes — and for defaulte of such yssue unto such person and persons and his and theire heires as shalbe their next heire unto the said Sir Wm Browne and my further mynde and intente ys that for the better mayntenance of all and every suche my sonnes as shall not be my eldest sonne and shall not be otherwise advanced by me before my decease and for the better advancement of my said daughters as shall not be likewise so advanced by me before my decease — That then the said Sir Wm Russell, Sir Robert Sydney, Peter Manwood, Thos Edmond, Rowland White and Philip Harison the

57

survivors of them and the heires of the Survivors of them shall first of all before any suche guiftes in tayle be made unto my said sonnes and daughters in manner as aforsaid give and graunte by sufficient afsurance in the Lawe unto every one of my said sonnes not beyng my eldest sonn and to every of my said daughters not otherwise beyng advanced one yerelie Rent of tenne Poundes of Englishe money yerelie goyng out of the premises payable quarterlie by equall porcons with sufficient clauses of distrefse in every of the said graunts to be conteyned for the better levying of every suche Rent charge as aforesaid to have and to hould every of the said Rents to every of my said sonnes and daughters respectivelie for terme of his her & their lives. And for the disposition of all my goodes and Chattells I constitute and make my said wife my sole Executrix she paying and performing all suche legacies as I shall set down in my Codicill unto this present testament to be annexed — In witness whereof unto theise presents I have set my hande and seale the two and twentieth daye of Septmber in the four and fortieth yere of the rayne of our Soveraigne Lady Elizabeth by the grace of God of England, ffrance & Ireland and Queene defender of the faithe —William Browne

Instead of a schedule, I have annexed this wryting to my will above specified that is that I bequeath unto each of my children (Except my eldest sonne living at the day of my death, one hundred and twenty pounds sterling, where with the better to maynteyne themselves, and yf my beloved wife, can otherwise without receyving the profitt of this maintayne herselfe and them — Then my hope and desire ys that yt may be employed to make up a greater somme towardes theire advancement in marriage or otherwise — And my desire & will is that when my eldest sonne shall come to be one and twenty yeares of age that then my wife shall allowe hym thirty pounds Sterling yearly but he not to have any one hundred and twenty poundes as the rest layed out for hym This is all written underneath the first draughte of my will and signed with my hand the seaventhe of Julie 1604 in the second yere of our Sacred Majestie King James

William Browne

These wordes tenne poundes of English money were enterlyned with my owne hand the Seventh of Julie 1604 for witnefse I have subscribed my hand the daye above written.

William Browne

Will proved by Mary Browne, relict, 23 of January 1611.—

-----------------------0-----------------------

Notes to the Will of Sir William Browne Knight.

-----------------------0-----------------------

Sir William Russell Kn^t was the 4th and youngest son of Francis - 2nd Earl of Bedford. He was knighted for his valour in Ireland, and greatly distinguished himself at the Battle of Zutphen in Holland. He was for several years Treasurer of the Navy and in 1603 created Baron of Thornbaugh by James 1st. His grandson Sir John Russell married Robert Lord Rich's widow, who was the youngest daughter of Oliver Cromwell. She died January 27th 1720, aged 83.

-----------------------0-----------------------

Sir Robert Sidney, on the 28th January 1588 entered into possession of all his brother's estates, and on 16 July of the same year was made Lord Governor of Flushing. He was sent not long after to the King of Scotland to compliment him on his respect to Queen Elizth for his attitude towards the Spanish Armada. In 1593 he was sent as ambassador to the King of France and in 1597 was joined in command with Sir Francis Vere, over the English Auxilliary Forces. His post of

Governor of Flushing was renewed & joined with the Government of the Castle of Ramekins by James 1st - 22 April 1603. By letters patent 13th May, he was raised to the dignity of Baron, as Lord Sydney. On 25 July he was made Lord Chamberlain to the Queen, and on the 4th May (3rd of James 1st) was created Viscount L'Isle. In 1613 he was appointed to conduct the Princess Elizabeth (married to Frederick Elector Palatine of Bohemia) to his dominions. The cautionary towns, on the solicitations of the States of Holland, by the payment of all cautionary & money charges, were delivered up by Lord Viscount L'Isle in 1616 & all the subordinate officers & soldiers &c were discharged. On July 7 1616, he was installed a Knight of the Garter and 2 August 1618 succeeded to the title of Earl of Leicester. "July 14 1626. On Saturday last the good Earl of Leicester having been at Court, going & returning by water to Baynard's Castle fell into an apoplexy and thereof yesterday between 11 & 12 noon, died, being in great debt. By his death one good pension of 1000 or 1200 £ falls in to the Exchequer."*

-----------------------0-----------------------

Sir Thomas Edmonds, was a celebrated diplomatist of the two preceding reigns (Elizth and James). He was born in Devonshire in 1563, resident at the Court of France in 1592, six years later was sent on a mifsion to the Archduke Albert, (Netherlands) and again as Ambassador in 1604. He was also ambassador to France on two other occasions, and held many other appointments at home. He died in 1639.

-----------------------0-----------------------

Roland Whyte, was the son of Griffith Whyte of Wales. He lived in the Earl of Pembroke's house at Baynard's Castle on terms of intimacy with

---

* Court and Times of Charles 1st.

the family & his connection with the Sydney's probably originated in their alliances with that nobleman. Sir Robt employed him as his solicitor at Court and paid him a salary to do that and write him news letters.

Sir Peter Manwood Kn^t of St. Stephens, Kent, near Canterbury, was the eldest son of Sir Roger Manwood, who was made Baron of the Exchequer in the early part of Queen Elizabeth's reign. Sir Peter represented Sandwich in several parliaments and was made a Knight of the Bath at the coronation of James 1st. He was not only learned himself, but a generous patron of learned men. He wrote the "Epistle dedicatory" to Sir Roger Williams' history of "The Action of the Low Countries" published in 1618. He died in 1625.

Sir Nathaniel Rich Kn[t]

Nathaniel Rich was the eldest son of Col. Nathaniel Rich of Stondon, Essex and Elizabeth the daughter of Sir Edmund Hampden of Buckinghamshire. His name is found in 1605, amongst the number of students at Emmanuel College Cambridge.[◊] This college was founded in 1587 by Sir Walter Mildmay and was regarded in those days as the nursery of Puritan scholars and preachers. Here the Rev[d] Thomas Hooker received his education, and afterwards emigrated to New England in 1633. The subject of our notice, seems to have had ill health through life, as sundry prescriptions of D[r] W. Mayerne's, preserved among his papers fully attest. In 1615, for instance, his ailments were, "gout and melancholy" and he had "directions to make clisters to suppresse melancholike fumes," & ordered "to dine at 10 o'clock, sup at 5 and eat but one dish at one meal." He probably carried his experiments in medicines too far, in reference to the "antimmoniall cupp or the universal medicine" for we find in a letter[X] of one Mathew Cradock to John Winthrop (London 15 March 1636) that "if I bee not misinformed the usse thereof (I feare immoderat) was an occasion of shortening Sir Nathaniel Rich's dayes, who hath made and Exchange of this liffe ffor a better." About the year 1616 Nathaniel Rich associated himself with Sir Rob[t] Rich in fitting out several commercial and exploring expeditions. They were both interested in the colonization of Virginia and the

---

[◊] For notes concerning Emmanuel College, see pages   and   .

[X] Massachusetts Historical Society's Collections.

Summer's Islands or Bermudas. In the Virginia Company, Sir Robert held stock to the amount of £75. Sir Robert Rich was the eldest son of the "rich" Lord Rich 1st Earl of Warwick, who married Penelope Deveraux, sister of the unfortunate Earl of Essex. Sir Robert on the death of his father, 28 March 1618/19 became 2nd Earl of Warwick.[*] He married Frances daughter & heiress of Sir Wm Hatton by Elizabeth — granddaughter & heiress of Sir Francis Gaudy. On the 8th of November 1617 Lady Hatton "the wife of Sir Edward Coke quondam Lord Chief Justice entertained the King (James 1st) — Buckingham and the rest of the Peers, at a splendid dinner, not inviting her husband."[A] On this occasion "his Majesty knighted at Hatton House, Sir Nathaniel Rich of London, Sir Francis Needham and Sir Peter Chapman. Lady Hatton was the daughter of the Earl of Exeter. Sir Nathaniel was a kinsman of Sir Robert Rich.[B] . . . In 1616 John Rolf (the husband of Pocahontas) wrote to Sir Robert Rich "a true relation of the State of Virginia" in which the settlement and its prospects are minutely described. Robert Rich the younger brother of Sir Nathaniel went out to this settlement in 1609 and returned to London in 1610 where he published the ballad "Newes from Virginia" and tells the reader "I am for Virginia againe and so I will bid thee hastily farewell with an honest verse,

"As I came hether, to see my native land,

"to waft me backe lend me thy gentle hands.

The "Summer Islands Company" seems to have been

---

[*] He was Lord High Admiral under the Commonwealth. He was the patron & friend of Hugh Peters.

[A] Camden Annals . . . .

[B] John Chamberlain's letter to Sir Dudley Carlton.

established as an independent enterprise as early as 1615 and the records of its existence extend, with some breaks, up to 1634. In the British Museum is preserved the letter book of this Company, containing 8 letters 1633 to 1636 written in cypher by Sir Nathaniel Rich, and signed by him, to Hugh Wentworth one of their commissioners out there. Lewis Hughes was the Minister sent over to the Islands and he succeeded in establishing the Presbyterian form of worship there by 1617. Daniel Tucker was the first Governor, but was soon recalled, and Capt Nathaniel Butler sent over in his stead. The latter was entirely directed to the interests of Sir Robert and Sir Nathaniel. In 1619 violent dissensions broke out amongst the directors of the Virginia Company and two hostile factions were soon arrayed against each other. On the one side were Sir Robt Rich (now Earl of Warwick) Sir Nathaniel Rich, Alderman Johnson and others, and the Earl of Southampton, Lord Cavendish and Sir Edward Sackville on the other. One party supported Sir Thomas Smith, who had been the Govr or Treasurer for the previous 12 years, and the other had for its candidate Sir Edwin Sandys who was elected. "May 8. 1619. The Virginia Company have displaced Sir Thomas Smith and made Sir Edwin Sandys their Govnr." But the matter is little amended: when the next court or meeting they confirmed Sir Thomas Smith in his presidentship of the Bermudas or Summer Islands for I could hardly tell how to resolve if it were put to my choice."[a] Much bickering continued in the Company until 1623 when Alderman Johnson suggested the presentation of a petition to inquire into the affairs of the Colony. A strong advocate of the settlers claims was found in Sir Nathaniel Rich who presented the matter to the House of Commons in 1624 in a speech,

---

[a] Letter of John Chamberlaine to Sir Dudley Coulton.

and finally obtained a Royal Commission of Enquiry. The effect was soon apparent for means went then to relieve the pressing wants of the colony as promptly as possible. Complaints had been made in 1623 and a list of the names of "adventurers that disliked the present proceedings of business in the Virginia and Summer Island Companies." They were 83 in number, as the Earl of Warwick, Sir N^l Rich, Sir Saml Argall, Sir Thos Wroth, Alderman Johnson &c &c. The Earl of Warwick and Sir Nathl Rich, becoming dissatisfied with the unproductive results of the Summer Islands Enterprise, fitted out a ship, in 1629 and made a successful voyage of discovery, under Capt Elfred. The suggestion was Capt Bells, who indicated the Existence of certain islands known as the St Kathalina & Foncata. The islands were renamed Providence Islands and Capt Elfred was placed there as the first Governor, but soon gave way to Capt Bell. A trading company was organized, and existed for several years. In May 23^d - 1639 the Earl of Warwick was elected the Governor of the Providence Comp^y John Pym Deputy Governor, and Will. Jessop Secretary at a Salary of 40£ a year. At this meeting the Governor preposed to sell the Island to the West India Company which was agreed to, and a declaration made that they were ready to treat for the sale. In this Company the Earl of Warwick had invested 2.430£ — Lord Mandeville (inheriting Sir Nathaniel Rich's shares) 2280£, and John Pym 3.185£. Besides having an interest in the West India Companies, Sir Nathaniel was one of the grantees of the Plymouth Company (of New England) Patent Novr 3^d - 1620. He promoted the colonization of the new settlements by the Puritans & manifested his interest in their welfare in various ways. His name is alluded to with great respect, by the early letter writers in New England, and his premature death in 1636 much lamented. The following letter was addressed by Sir Nathaniel Rich to his old tutor Dr Wm Sancroft who eventually became the 3rd Master of

Emmanuel College. He was uncle to Wm Sancroft, a fellow of Emmanuel and afterwards, its master & made Archbishop of Canterbury in 1665.

Good Sir . . . I hartely thanke you for your kind remembrance of me in yor letter and the paper therein enclosed wherein I tooke much contentment though I confefs I am sorry that we should be now driven to search out Arguments against these things, which are too much honoured & countenanced, even by calling them into disputes: Our comfort is that Truth, will in the end prevayle against and become more glorious by opposition but yett nothing in comparison of that eternall triumph wch it will one day have in heaven and then will all her friends triumph with her and none so much as those y^t have contended and endured most in her quarrell. In which respect your self (amongst many others who syde with God and his truth in theise tymes) are in this particular happy above others that God hath given you not only eminent abilityes & prudent courage to serve him in this kind, but that many (too many) occasions are frequently present to draw them forth into action & in my poore opinion are like to be daylie more & more. And this is one of those good things wch the only wise God expects out of bold & imprudent will and error even the honour of his own graces in the harts of his children thereby the more excited to conflict & repell them. You may remember w^t I wished (when I was last with you) might be the Motto of E͞manuell Colledge, wch I doe & allwayes shall pray may be versified of it: Tu ne cede malis sed contrâ audentior ito: Sir I have herewith sent you the Booke wch I promised you wch you should sooner have had, could I sooner have procured it. desyringe you that wherein soever I may seeme to be of any use unto you yo^u would freely co͞mand me as one that doe truly love & honour y^r worth and would be most glad to find the meanes of expressing myselfe.

Y^r very assured freind to serve you   Na Rich

From Warwick House in Holborne this 20th Novem^r 1633.

I pray when yo^u see the good Doctor Chaderton remember me kindly unto him." The letter endorsed "to my very worthy freind Mr Doctor Sancroft Master of Emmanuel College in Cambridge" (Note) "good Dr Chaderton" was chosen by Sir Walter Mildmay to be the 1st Master of Emmanuel. He was a Fellow of Christ's College. He lived to be 103 years old, but resigned the Mastership in 1622 having held the office for 38 years but continued to reside in the college where he died in 1640 & was buried in the college chapel.

In the 18th year of the reign of James 1st — Parliament met on the 18th January (1620). Sir Nathaniel Rich had been elected a member for Harwich, and thus commenced his parliamentary career, which extended over eight years. On the 15th February 48 members were chosen for the Privy Council, and Sir Nathaniel's name is found amongst the number. On looking over the proceedings of the House of Commons from 1620 to 1628, his name is constantly met with on committees, in connection with John Pym's & Hampden's. He was one of the most constant in his attendance, of the members, spoke frequently and much to the point, and was particularly happy in quoting precedents, in the many collisions, the House had with the King. He took a leading part in the impeachment of Buckingham and in the different moves that led up to it. So displeased was the King with this party of obstruction that Rushworth says "The King was highly displeased with some of the Common house, whom he called "ill tempered spirits." Sir Dudley Diggs, Sir Thos Crew, Sir Nathaniel Rich, Sir James Perrot, Sir Thos Blundell, Sir John Jephson, and Sir Thomas Penruddock, were sent over to Ireland, for punishment, joined in commission under the Great Seal of England for the enquiry of sundry matters concerning his Majesty's service, as well in the

Government, Ecclesiastical & civil, as in points of Revenue &c." — "Each commissioner was allowed 30 shillings a day to begin from the 20 Feb^y, and every one hath 100£ delivered him afoot and by way of imprefs." They proceeded to Ireland in March 9th 1621/22.... The King in 1620-1 endeavoured to induce the House, to sanction active measures for securing Bohemia to his daughter & her husband and the young Palatine, who had been driven off his throne by a rising of his subjects. Sir James Perrot & Sir Thos Wentworth supported such measures & asked the house to make a declaration to that effect, but it would not do so, whereupon cried out Sir Edwd Cecil & Sir Nathaniel Rich, (as the minute was made in the clerks book) "Rather this declaration than 10.000 men on the march."

In the Parliament of 1624-5 Sir Nathaniel was elected both for Retford and Harwich, and on February 15th the Countefs of Devonshire wrote to him asking him to transfer the Burghership of Retford to her son, who had sat for that place in a previous Parliament. This he did and remained the member for his former constituency.

June 25th 1625. Concerning the enlarging of preaching, Sir Nathaniel Rich moved "that silent ministers may be allowed to preach in all points agreeable to the doctrine and discipline of the Church of England. The like petition hath bene (almost) in every Parliament. They refuse not to subscribe to the articles according to the statute, but another subscription is required by cannon: and noe cannon can compell a man under a penaltye to loose his freehold." The question was then debated at length.

John Pym had brought before the attention of the House Rich and Montagues "book of meditation to reconcile us to the Papists." The tendency of these books had been debated and on the 9th July (1625) "The question concerning Montague was quickly settled and accordinge to the motion of Sir Nathaniel Rich that to give his Majestie satisfaction, Mr Sollicitor might inform him that it was the opinion of the Commons that the booke is a seditious and seducinge booke & deserved a publicke censure but that wee should not release him only enter an order for the Serjeant to let him out upon Bonds."

On August 6th 1625 — the question of subsidy had been keenly debated for several sittings, when Sir John Eliot rose with a proposition for an address to the King for permifsion to continue to sit. He was followed by Sir Nathaniel Rich who said "Some move to give and give presentlie and some would not give at all and some would give sub-modo and a fourth to which he inclineth was to propound fyve hedds, which he desyred might be referred to a committee to frame into a petition, wherein the Kinges answere would yield a great satisfaction to the countrye though they could not be all perfected now & that answere beinge obteyned we shal be the fitter to resolve the question of supply.

1st. Concerning religion: The Isrealites could not prosper so long as the execrable thinge was amonge them: wee have as little hope of successe as longe as idolatry is so common. But wee alreadye expect the Kinges answere for this which hee desyred might be in Parliament & then it shall have the force of a lawe.

2nd.. That wee may know the enemye

3rd .. That it would please his Majestie to use grave counsellors in the government of those grave affaires.

4th That we might at our next meetinge have sufficient tyme to looke into the King's Estate, that so hee might be enabled to subsist of himselfe.

5th The desyer of his Majesties answere concerninge the impositions. . . .

If it be objected wee shall not have tyme enough, the course anciently was to present the heds of their petition and to Expect an answere at the next meetinge: others may objecte that hereby wee shall Capitulate with the Kinge. 22nd Edward 3^d the Commons gave three 15^s upon 2 conditions: 1st That if the warr did cease the guifte ought to be voyde. 2nd That his Majesties answere to their petitions might be inrolde." This speech was afsailed at once by Edward Clarke, a connection of Buckingham's who said that "Invectives with bitternefs are unreasonable for this time." Sir Robert Philips commended the platform of Sir Nathaniel Rich and sayd that wee were beholding unto him for shewing us the way which hee desyred wee would thinke of againe and in the meantime drawe them into heades." After Mr Clarke had spoken the above, he was stopt & commanded to Explaine which he did, but without any submifsion or excuse and thereupon sent out of the House & ordered that he should stand committed to the Serjeant till the further pleasure of the House might be knowen: and being called agayne to the barr, kneelinge Mr Speaker told him the Order of the House."

The House received a message from the King, that the next sitting of the Commons would be held at Oxford two days after.

8th May - 1626. In the impeachment of Buckingham Sir Nathaniel Rich, Sir William Armine and Nine others acted as assistants in the House whilst Sir Dudley Diggs took the part of leader. He opened the proceedings by a speech, and was in no way daunted by the presence of the Duke of Buckingham. The House met again after dinner, after having passed a vote for the imprisonment of the Duke — by 225 votes for and 105 against. Sir Nathaniel Rich was appointed messenger to convey the information to the House of Lords. This was decided upon on a Wednesday, but it was deemed best not to send the messenger into the Lords until Thursday. Sir John Eliot delivered a speech on the subject of the Imprisonment, of which one of the members (nameless) said "This was as bold and worthy a speech as ever I heard, onlie a little too tart." Forster calls it "a phillipic of the bitterest order." The King had as many as 4 or 5 note takers whilst Eliot was speaking. On Thursday morning when Sir Nathaniel Rich had returned from delivering his message Sir Dudley Diggs and Sir John Eliot were gone from the House. They had been called out "by one at the door" and carried to the Tower, whereupon the house broke off all business. When the House met on Friday the 12th, the Speaker offering to proceed to the business of the day, he was silenced by cries of "Sit down, Sit down, no business till we are righted in our liberties." Sir Dudley Diggs was released the next day but Sir John Eliot was kept a prisoner until the 20th of May.

In the election for the Parliament of 1627, the opponents of the Court were generally successful. Sir Nathaniel Rich again represented Harwich — John Pym — for Tavistock & John Hampden for Wendover. The Parliament of 1626 was dissolved on the 15th June, and the newly elected one met on the 17th March 1627. On the 20th of that month a committee of 86 members was appointed and called the "Committee of Privileges to consider and Examine all questions growing out of Elections, Returns and other privileges of the House/" and on this Committee Sir Nathaniel Rich served.

In 1628 the House had granted a subsidy the King asked for, but would name no time and Sir Edward Coke wished it being Good Friday, it would be a good deed to fix the period for its coming into operation. But Sir John Eliot strenuously resisted. The matter was however referred to a Committee at which Sir Nathaniel Rich carried a proposal to limit the term of one year from that date, addition being afterwards made, by way of reply to the King's message that no further suggestion as to supply from any quarter would be entertayned until the question relating to the liberty of the subject should be finally determined."

5th June 1628. King Charles 1st sent the House a message that he had set a day to terminate the session and commanded the speaker to let them know he would hold that day prefixed without alteration and enjoined them not to enter upon any new business. After Sir John Eliot had spoken and Sir Dudley Diggs had said "I am as much grieved as ever, must we not proceed? let us sit in silence, we are miserable, we know not what to do." Hereupon there was a sad silence (Rushforth says) in the House for a while which was broken by Sir Nathaniel Rich in these words "we must now speak, or forever hold our peace: for us to be silent when King and Kingdom are in this calamity, is not fit. The question is whether we shall secure ourselves by silence. Yea or no? I know it is more for our own security but is it not for the security of those for whom we serve, let us think on them. Some instruments desire a change, we fear his Majesty's safety & the safety of the Kingdom. I do not say we now see it, and shall we now sit still and do nothing and so be scattered? Let us go together to the Lords and show our dangers that we may then go to the King together."

After the dissolution of the Parliament of 1629 there was no meeting of the Commons until 1640. As Lord Clarendon observes "that the unhappy assaults made upon the Prerogatative had produced the untimely dissolution of the last & the King was resolved, now, to try if he could not give his people a taste of Happiness & let them see the Equity of his Govern^t in a single State." —

Oxford 8th August 1625. "Sir Robert Nye had informed the house that Mr Clarke was readye at the dore, humbly desyringe to be admitted to make his submissions. Thereupon he was called in and at the barr made a confession of his faulte, kneelinge & protestinge that hee had rather dye a thousand deathes then disturbe the peace of our proceedings, and beinge sent out againe the House agreed that he should be discharged, which the Speaker signified unto him beinge againe brought to the Barr, but not Kneelinge. A messenger came from the Lordes that the King had commanded my Lord of Buckingham to deliver divers matters to both Houses and they were desyred to meet the Lordes in the afternoone in Christ Church Hall. This message bred some doubt for if this meetinge were of both Houses the Speaker ought to goe and all the members to be covered. Some propounded to Send to the Lordes for an Exposition of the message; but that was misliked because it came from the Kinge and it might be thought no discretion in us to desyer them to Expound the Kings message, Sir Nathaniel Rich said — "The Speaker not to goe but when the Kinge is present in person or by commission Anciently the Lords were wont to come downe into this House to acquainte us with businefse till 2^d Richard 2^d when they Excepted against that course, but afterward it was restored agayne till Henry 6th, when the Lordes sent to the Commons to meete with them which they refused and the difference was referred to the Kinges pleasure who ordered that they should not come but with protestation that it was of favour, not of duty. In 3 & 6 Henry 8th divers great lordes came into this House accordinge to the auncient manner. But the Lordes havinge private notice of this difficultye sent another message declaringe that their former messenger had mistaken their instruction for their desyer was that the meetinge might be by the Committees of both Houses, so that debate was ended.' The meeting was ordered and Sir Edward Coke, Mr Sollicitor, Mr Recorder, Sir Dudley Diggs, Sir Nathaniel Rich, and Mr Pym appoynted to make the reporte.

–Robert Rich–

Robert Rich was the younger brother of Sir Nathaniel Rich, who embarked for Jamestown Virginia in 1609 in the Ship Sea Venture, in Company with Sir Thomas Gates and Sir Geo. Somers. The vessel was wrecked on a reef of the Bermudas Islands, but he returned to London in 1610 as we find from his address "to the reader" prefixed to his Ballad "Newes from Virginia'. He calls himself a "soldier, blunt and plaine," and says he must start again for Virginia, in order that "I must not loose my patrymonie." His brother Nathaniel was a shareholder in the Virginia Company, and he himself held £12.10 in the venture. He went out again in 1610 to the Summer Islands, or the Bermudas, and engaged in the cultivation of tobacco and other produce. Lewis Hughes the clergyman stationed in the Islands in writing to Sir N^l Rich praises the Exertions of Robert Rich who was "distributing to every man his due" out of the provision "sent over by Sir Robert Rich." In one of his letters Robt calls Lewis Hughes his "Especial friend and bed fellow." In 1617 Sir Nathaniel bought of John Hamor ten of his shares in the Summers Isl^d Comp^y for his brother. Thomas Durham writing in 1619 to Sir Nathaniel from the Islands considered Robert Rich "too good natured' and gave a warning against allowing the practice of his, of planting a "wife's crop of tobacco." An answer came in reply from the Earl of Warwick & Sir N^l Rich "that with woman's tobacco, they will women all." The above remark about the "wife's crop" would imply that Robt Rich had his wife with him on the Island. Then comes a letter from John Hamor (September, 24. 1620) announcing the death of his brother to Sir

Nathaniel, and on Octr 18 another from Thos Durham lamenting that Robert Rich had been treated by Edward Athen after the manner of "a blind physician, or rather a quacksalver" and he seems very indignant at the conduct of Robert's Executor because he "had not the honesty or manners to invite Mr Kendall & Mr Semer who gave Mr Rich a volley of shot at his burial to so much as a cup of aqua-vitae or anything else, according to the ancient and laudable custom" and desires his brother in London to have the coat of arms of the deceased drawn by the Herald's College, and sent out for the purpose of having a solemn funeral performed." He left two sons, Nathaniel, who inherited his uncle Nathaniels Estate in Stondon, Essex, and Robert of Rose hall, Beccles Suffolk, who married Mary, the second daughter of Sir Charles Rich Bart, the son of Sir Edmund Rich Bart of Norfolk. By her he had a fortune of £20.000. Sir Robert served in several parliaments for Dunwich. He succeeded, 16 May 1677 to the dignity of Baronet & in the estate of Sir Charles Rich. Sir Robt had Charles who died without issue & Robert besides 3 other sons and 8 daughters. He died 1. Oct. 1699, and was succeeded by Sir Robert his eldest surviving son. He was one of the grooms of the bed chambers to his late Majesty, served in several Parliaments & went through the Army with great honours, and finally became Senior Field Marshall. He died 1. Feb. 1768 and was succeeded by his eldest son Robert, who married the daughter of the Honble Mr Ludlow brother to the right Honble Peter Earl of Ludlow and had issue an only daughter. She married Chas Bostock of C^o Meath Ireland, who in 1790 assumed the name & arms of Rich & was in 1791 created a Baronet. Issues 6 sons & 6 daughters. There is much of poetical interest connected with the voyage of the "Sea Venture," in 1609, and her shipwreck on the Bermudas.[*] The favorable circumstances of the wreck, the semi-tropical character of the Island, with its beautiful vegetation, the sturdy nature of old Sir George Somers, the birth of Bermuda Rolfe & the boy Bermudas — the idyllic life of their enforced residence of nearly a year — and the building of the two pinnaces of cedar "with little or no yron at all", which Robert Rich brings into his verse

> And there two gallant pynaces
> Did build of seader-tree
> The brave Deliverance, one was called
> Of seaventy tonne was shee
> The other, Patience had to name
> Her burthen thirty tonne
> Two only of their men which there
> Pale death did overcome.

It is moreover, most interesting to have the testimony of an eyewitness of the sailing of the "Sea Venture" and her consorts. Sir Stephen Powle (or Powell) Knight, was a gentleman of the long robe, and clerk of the Crown, who had invested £100 in the fortunes of the Virginia Company. So he was induced to come down to the waterside to see the Fleet set sail, and then made the following entries in a commonplace book, which he had commenced the 9° October 1597.

---

[*] "Among the many charms which Bermuda has for a poetic eye, we cannot for an instant forget that it is the scene of Shakspeare's Tempest; and that here he conjured up the "delicate Ariel" who alone is worth the whole heaven of ancient mythology." From Moores Epistles, Odes and other Poems London 1806 Page 42 Epistle III.

Memorandum 9° March 1608

Betweene the howers of 10 and 11 in the forenoone the day and yeare above written I delivered to Sir Thomas Smith Treasurer of the viage to Virginia the summe of fifty poundes in mony towlde for which I received a noate with the Armes of England testifyinge the receipt thereof an am to be one of the Counsell of this expedition, my name allso was inserted into the rowles and booke Kept by M^r ————. The successe of which undertakinge I referre to God Allmighty.

15 Maij. – 1609. On Monday in the morninge oure 6 shippes lyinge at Blackwall wayed anker and fell down to beginne the viage toward Virginea. Sir Thomas Gates beinge the deputy Governour untill the Lord Delaware doth comme the other which is supposed shalbe about two months hence. Captayne H Neport, Captayne Sir George Sommers and 800 people of all sortes went in these 6 shippes besydes two moare that attend the fleete at Plymouth and ther be inhabitants allready at Virginea, about 160. God bless them, and guide them to his glory and our goode — Amen.

13th February 1609 being Tuesday Sir Thos Roe our commander for the discovery of Guiana and Sir George Brooke (as I hearde since) departed for Dartmouth wheare oure 2 shippes and provisions for 2 pinnesses more bestowed in them lay at wate for his comminge partenerrs. The Earle of Sowthampton 900£, Sir Walter Rawley 600£, Sir Thos Roe himselfe with his parteners £1100, and mysealf £20, which viage god bless. The two shippes departed from Dartmouth the 24 of February 1609.

Y^e March 9 - 1609 — The Lord Delaware tooke his leave of all the Company on Monday at Sir Thomas Smith's in Fillpott Lane Treasurer of the Virginea Company; and on Satturday following — 10th Martij he departed towardes his howse in Hampshire from whence he

77

went to meete his shippe at Sowthampton readdy furnished with stores, and plantes, seedes, and all other provision of graynes as well to sowe as to vittaile one thousande men for one yeare. He has three shippes, one whear him sealfe was, of 200 tunne called the ———— a Flyboate of 400 tunnes, and a pinace of 120 tunnes. His style was Lord Governour and Captayne of Virginea. He tooke shippinge for that viage the — of —. God blesse his worthy endeavour.

————————O————————

Names of the adventurers, with the several sums adventured, paid to Sir Thomas Smith, Knight, late Treasurer of the Company for Virginia, and persons who are mentioned in his volume.

————————O————————

William Browne------------------------------ £ 12.10.0

Robert Sydney Lord Lisle

now Earl of Leicester----------------------------- 90.0.0

Sir Peter Manwood--------------------------------50.0.0

William, Earl of Pembroke-----------------------400.0.0

Sir Stephen Powell (or Powle)------------------ 100.0.0

Sir Robert Rich now

Earl of Warwick------------------------------------75.0.0

Sir William Russell--------------------------------50.0.0

Robert Rich--12.10.0

Sir Thomas Smith--------------------------------145.0.0

Sir Horatio Vere--------------------------------- 121.0.0

Sir Robert Wroth--------------------------------- 50.0.0

————————O————————

Col. Nathaniel Rich

Col Nathaniel Rich was the only son of Robert Rich and was born in the Summer Islands after the death of his father in 1620, his education was taken charge of by his uncle Sir Nath[l] Rich who placed him under the tuition of the Rev[d] M[r] Wharton at Felsted, Essex. Here he remained until he went up to Cambridge, probably to Emmanuel College. He no doubt went through a course of law in Lincoln's Inn, as his uncle in his will instructs his Executor "to allow him ffowerscore pounds per annum for his education for some time at the University of Cambridge, & then at Lincoln's Inn it being my desire that he should study & profess the Law." He became Admiralty Commissioner in 1643 & the House of Commons "approved him as Colenal in Sir Thos Fairfax's army in 1644." The following letter was addressed to Sir Tho[s] Barrington who had married into the Rich family. Oct 14. 1643. "Flyford. we are now this morning advancing towards Newark, conceiving it the most considerable garrison the enemy hath of the two viz. it and Gainsborough. The winter is already come and our lying in the field hath lost us more men than have been taken away either by sword or bullet: notwithstanding which (and many of our men lying scattered up and down the country) we are ready to persist and unwilling to wait any opportunity of doing God honour and our country service: yet if God pleases to bring us safe to our winter quarters you must think of speedy recruiting our troops which are not a little battered and lessened with what service we have done." He says the soldiers complain of want of pay and that he and his troops are 9 weeks behind hand. "All the money that I had but 30 odd pounds I gave them while I had it (which I saved for my own necessities in case of being wounded or sick or the like distrefs) and that was stolen off from my horse when we lay in the field before Lincoln and at that time I had but two shillings left me and my troop without money and have rested so ever since and long before and if speedy relief is not sent with which our sick soldiers lying here and these without subsistence and those that are well, being continued upon actual service without encouragement, I am afraid ere long you will be as willing to raise new troops or recruit the old: if we had free quarters wherever we come yet a soldier being with out any money, his horse cannot be shod, or his arms or saddle kept fix, what I speak is in behalf of the common soldiers, not officers. . . . Therefore I beseech you let the common soldiers be constantly paid th^o the officers go without any at all.

Nathaniel Rich

A letter from Walmer Castle 9 July 1648 addressed by Col Rich to the House of Commons was read by the Speaker, and another on the 10th July to the Committee of Kent, when it was "ordered that it be referred to a Committee of the Army, to consider how Powder & other Provisions may be speedily sent to Col Rich." Another from him of the 18th August (1648) was read in the House of Commons and ordered to be forthwith printed. It was also "Ordered that a Letter of Thanks to be signed by Mr Speaker be sent to Col Rich acknowledging his very good service against the Enemy that intended to raise the Siege at Deale Castle." A sum of money was also voted to be paid Col Rich "out of the new sequestrations in Kent." The House also gave orders to hand him his means of pay.

Under date of August 25th 1648 Col Rich writes to William Lenthall Esq Speaker of the House of Commons, from Deale that since the surrender of Walmer Castle, "no time has been lost to use all means possible to reduce Deale Castle," He reports the Capture of this Castle, with much store of ammunition &c and sends Lt Col Axtell, as bearer of dispatches & Commands him as having been "Extraordinary active and diligent." He will next invest Sundown Castle of which he hopes to give "allso a good account in a few dayes." The Council of State, May 21st 1653, appoint Col Nathaniel Rich and others to consider the present condition of the Summer Islands. Sir David Kirk in 1638 surreptitiously obtained a patent of Newfoundland and in 1655, (after disposessing Cecil Lord Baltimore of all his rights there) made over part of his patent to John Claypole (son in law to Cromwell) Col Rich and others. "1657. September 30. Oliver Cromwell to the Honble Col Rich at Liverpool — I do well assure you that before this I sent you an order to be afsistinge in the Expedition against the Isle of Man: but hearinge nothing from you I doubt whether my order came to you. But now I thought fitt to send this desire that (Col Lisburne beinge employed another way) you would be afsisting to Col Duckinfield in this service whoe is the Commander in Chiefe. I rest your loving friend

O. Cromwell

About a year before (12 September 1656) Col Rich was denounced as one of "the new malignants" or fifth monarchy men, with Vane, Harrison and others, and had been kept a prisoner at Windsor for several weeks. John Evelyn in his Diary mentions that 22nd of April (1656) "afterwards I went to see his Majesty's house at Eltham, both Palace and Chapell in miserable ruines, the noble woods and park destroy'd by Rich the Rebell." In 1659 Col Rich was returned a member of the House of Commons and on the 9th of July of that year, they approved of his appointment as a Colonel of a regiment of Horse. His commission was delivered to him in the House of Commons 15 July. On the 29th December (1659) the House "Resolved that the Thanks of this House be

81

given to Colonel Rich for his good service done for the Parliament and Commonwealth, and Mr Speaker did give Colonel Rich the Thanks of this House for his good service accordingly." Complaints and informations were again March 1659/60 lodged against Col Rich and Sir Arthur Hastlerigge. The House of Commons 7th March 1659/60 Resolved that Colonel Rich be called in.

"Mr Annesly reports from the Council of State, a letter from Col Ingoldsby from Bury, dated the 5th March 1659 and an Information given by Cornet Robert Thorneback against Colonel Rich which were read

"Col Rich standing up in his place, denied the charge laid against him and said he is a stranger to all represented.

"Resolved that the Parliament doth approve of what the Council of State have done, concerning the Commitment of Colonel Rich and bringing him to the Parliament being a member of the House.

Ordered that it be referred to the Council of State further to examine the whole matter charged against Colonel Rich and what else concerneth the Business, and forthwith to state matter of Fact and report it to the Parliament.

Resolved that Colonel Rich be, and is hereby injoined to attend the Council of State from time to time, upon the Examination of this Businefs."

James Holbrooke presents a petition to Secretary Nicholas "for directions for further securing Col Nathaniel Rich committed to his custody January 10, 1661, last also for relief as to his charges: he will not pay any fee, is conveying away his estate, refuses the oath of allegiance and has all sorts of people coming to him." Humphrey Lee informs Katharine Hurlestone that he is led by allegiance to inform against those in the Fleet (at Portsmouth) to whose Custody Col Nathaniel Rich was committed that he has liberty to go abroad when he likes and has stayed away nine dayes at a time though of most dangerous principles" —— November 17: 1663 Portsmouth, "Philip Honeywood Commander of the garrison readily grants Sir John Lawson's request. Found Col Rich and his lady in great hopes of more freedom by his meanes, the sad air and unwholesome water prejudice his health and prevent his enjoying his children and managing his estate. He says he has not disturbed Government since the Act of Indemnity and that were he at liberty he would live quietly and give bond for his appearance. He will not say whether he would take the oath of allegiance." A warrant was issued June 6, 1665 to Sir John Robinson, to receive Col N[l] Rich in the Tower of London from Portsmouth, and on July 18th, he was released, having given the necessary bonds to the Earl of Falmouth, in London.

The last public mention of Col Rich is in September 23, 1667. He doubtlefs retired to Stondon, which he had inherited from his uncle Sir Nathaniel, and led a quiet life for the rest of his days. He made his will October 21st 1700, which was signed March 3rd 1701: and proved sometime during 1702. In his will he says he has been married to his wife (2nd) Lady Elizabeth for 35 years, alludes to a promise respecting her, made to the Earl of Lothian —— names his son Nathaniel, and grandchild Nathaniel, son of his son Sir Robert and in default of heirs male, leaves property to the daughters of his son Nathaniel." Stondon remained in the Rich family until the time of Nathaniel Rich who married Mary daughter of Mathew Rudd of Little Badow in 1806. Nath[l] Rich who was for many years Receiver General of the Land Tax of the County sold this estate.

<u>Registro Curiae praerogat Cant Extract.</u>

Briefe containing my Resolution for the disposing of my Estate according to the Substance whereof I intend if God give me life and leifure to draw up my last Will and Testament which if I should be disappointed in, I appoint that this shalbe in the nature of a Will and that all my Lands Goods and Chattells shall be disposed according to the tenor of the partitioners hereunder menconed This being made the Second day of December 1635.—

First I will that all former Wills heretofore by me made shall be utterly void for that the same are not according to my mind and meaning — My soul I bequeath and commend to God my ffather in Jesus Christ — My body to be privately buryed in the night without any ffuneralls pomp or Mourning. The place I leave to the discretion of my Executors the R. H‾oble the Lord Mandevill whom I nominate and appoint sole Executor of my last Will and Testament but if convenient y^t maybe I would be buryed at Stondon in Essex in the parish Church there Only I would have my Executor Erect some Monument for me where ever I be buryed, the same not exceeding the summe of ffifty pounds or a hundred marks. — I would only have my Sisters and Brothers in Law and their Children and all my Servants to have mourning Suits of Black cloath. My mannor of Stondon and all my Lands in Essex I give to my Nephew Nathaniel Rich when he comes to the age of one and Twenty years — In the meane time my Executor to receive the Rent and to allow him ffowerscore pounds per Annum for his education for some time at the University of Cambridge and then at Lincoln's Inn — It being my desire that he should study and profess the Law — I give the profit of seven of my Shares in the Barmudaes now called the So‾mer Ilands to my sister Grimsdiche and her husband during their lives if they will goe and inhabite upon them — and one hundred and ffifty pounds in money for the transporting of themselves and such of their Children as they shall think fitt to carry with them.

I give one other share to my nephew Robert Browne now

84

residing in the said So ‾mer Islands, he having one other share there already upon the guift of my sister Wroth lately deceased — I give one other share thereof to —— Browne one other of the sons of my sister Browne deceased, who hath been hitherto educated by my noble ffriend the Countefs of Leicester, Mother to Sir John Smith — The residue of my Shares these being five I give for the maintenance of a ffree School in those Islands which my desire is should first be erected out of the profits of said five shares by the direction of my Executor and then laid forever to the said school — The Schoole master to be nominated and chosen by my Executor and his noble Lady and after their decease by such religious and discreet ffeoffees as they shall appoint — my desire is that some of the Indian Children to be brought either from Virginia or New England or some other Continent of America such as my Executor shall think fittest may be brought over there to be instructed in the Knowledge of true Religion, and to the end that my Executor may better perform the Trust comitted to him in the disposing of all the said Shares I doe give the Inheritance and ffreehold of them all to his Lo^{rp}, praying the Honourable Court of Adventurers for those Islands That imediately after my decease he may be admitted to them To have and to hold to him and his heires forever Neverthelefs upon the Trusts formerly mentioned and not anywayes to his own selfe But that in case my said Brother in Law Mr Grimsdich and his wife will not within one year after my decease go thither in their own persons, to live there Then I will not that neither of them have any benefit by this Guift unlefs by the hand of God they shall be hindred But that in that case my Executor take the yearly profits of those Shares and imploy the money raised thereby for three yeares towards the erection of the said ffree school And then pafs over the Inheritance of the said seven shares to such child or children of my said Brother and Sister Grimsditch as he shall conceive to be most worthy and also I co͞mit the Guift of the Inheritance of the said shares to be disposed of for the benefit of such child or children by my Executor in case they shall goe and live there after their decease, My meaning being that my said Brother in Law and his wife should have the use of those seven shares during their lives in case they live there, else not But in noe case to dispose of the Inheritance. The care whereof I leave wholly to my Executor for the good and benefit of their Children, especially such as by their vertue, diligence, and good course of life shall deserve best. I give to Nathaniel Browne now in New England with Mr Hooker the two hundred pounds which by my sister Morgan's Will was bequeathed unto him — and ffifty pounds more as my guift — which two-hundred and ffifty pounds I would have Mr Hooker imploy during the minority of the said Nathaniel Browne for and towards his education paying himselfe for his charges — This I would have done within one yeare after my decease — ITEM. I give unto Samuel Browne one other son of my sister Browne, one hundred pounds in money — The same to be imployed during his minority for his benefit as my Executor shall think most fitt. The Rectory of Neverne in Pembrokshire in Wales I give to my said Executor and his heirs forever upon this Trust and Confidence that he shall make sale thereof as soon as conveniently he can and dispose the money arising by sale thereof and of the Rents till it be sold for the performance of this my last Will and Testament. I give unto Thomas Grimsditch the eldest son of my brother Grimsditch who is now in the Isle of Providence, the fforty pounds per Annum Annuity which my Lord of Warwick is to pay during the life of the said Thomas — I give to Thomas Allaby my servant, one hundred pounds — To Jonas Anger Ten pounds per Annum during his life — The said Ten pounds per annum to be ifsuing out of my mannor of Stondon with power to distress & a nominie pence of six pence diem every day that it shall be unpaid within thirty dayes after Michaelmas and our Lady day, my meaning being that it whall be paid to him halfe yearly at the said ffeasts — And I give him Ten pounds in money — I give unto John my ffootman Ten Pounds in money and fforty shillings a year during his life Issuing out of the said Mannor To be paid halfe yearly as the other and with like power to distrefs and nominie pence not of vi^d a day but of twelve pence a week for every week that it shall be behind unpaid. All my Goods, Chattels, Leases of what kind or nature soever not formerly disposed of other then such Legacies as heretafter I shall exprefs either by word before two credible witnefses or by handwriting I give to my said Executor and his most noble Lady in testimony of my thankfulnefs unto them for all their favours and of the humble and hearty affection I justly bear unto them. I give unto William Jesopp more then formerly in my life I have given him ffifty pounds — All my wearing Lynnen and apparell I desire my Executor to distribute amongst my Brother Grimsditch and my servants according to his own discretion wherein I would have Thomas Allabie that waits on me especially respected, only one suit such as my Executor shall think fitt I give to William Jesopp And whereas there is in Mr Goffes hand (that was some time Steward to my Lord of Warwick) a statute taken in his name for a Thousand pounds debt due to my said Lord and my selfe, ffive hundred pounds whereof being the one halfe belongs to me I doe hereby give unto that my deare and noble Lord the said ffive hundred pounds as a testimony of my humble affection to him and thankfulnefs for his love and favours towards me, ITEM I give unto the R^t Hono^{ble} my Noble Lord the Earle of Holland One hundred pounds — and another hundred pounds to his noble Lady part of the money which his Lordship oweth me — and ffifty pounds parcell of the said Debt to my Noble Lady the Lady Essex Cheek — The Dyamond Ring which I usually weare it being my Sister Wroth's Legacie to me I give to my Brother Wroth — My

Emerod Ring which I usually weare I give to my dear and most vertuous friend Mrs Mary Moore widow — Item I do particularly give to my dear most noble and Religious Lady the Lady Mandevill All that Annuity of One hundred and ffourscore pounds per Annum which I purchased of my Lord of Warwick ifsueing out of Certain Lands in Norfolk during the minority of Mr Hatton Rich for all the terme of years which are yet to come — My Library, Bookes and papers I give to my said Noble Lord the Lord Mandevill the sole Executor of this my last Will and Testament, praying him that at least with part of them he would furnish a Library to be sett up in the ffree School at the So‾mer Ilands as formerly I have appointed The late Lady Warwick's picture I give unto my Lord Riche her son — Item I give unto my worthy friend Mr Wharton Minister at ffelsted in Essex Thirty pounds as a testimony of my speciall love unto him and thankfulnefs for his care bestowed in the education of my nephew Nathaniel Rich — ITEM I give unto my dear friend Mr John Pym my best Gelding and a Ring of twenty pounds which I desire him to weare for my sake — I give unto my loveing Cosen Mrs Martha Willford Twenty pounds to bestow in a Ring or what she please as a remembrance of my love unto her — And to the end that my Noble Lord whom I make sole Executor of this my last Will and Testament may be subject to the lefs trouble in the performance of this my Will I doe hereby declare my will and meaning to be That none unto whom I have given anything by this Will shall take any benefit thereby or have any thing thereby bequeathed unlefs at the same time that my Executor doe offer payment unto any such person of any such Legacie according to the Exprefs word, of this my Will he or she to whom the said Legacie is tendered due upon demand of my said Executor tender likewise a generall acquittance and discharge to my said Executor of all further claimes and demands whatsoever for or concerninge myselfe or anything pretended to be further claimed by from or under me or my said Executor as Executor of this my last Will and Testament — In Witnefs whereof and that this is my last Will and Testament though written in much haste I have subscribed to every page my name — And all the premises are written with my own hand Sed° Decembris 1635, Na: Riche. . . . . This and noe other was acknowledged by the said Sir Nathaniel Rich Knight being in full and perfect memory to be his last Will and Testament about the twenty Eighth of October 1636 before us vizt

Thomas Wolrych

Carey Wolrych.

M^d . . that on Thursday the Tenth day of November Anno D^{ni} 1636 after the sealing and publishing of the Will and Testament of Sir Nathaniel Riche Knight dated the second day of November 1635 The said Sir Nathaniel Riche did in the presence of the Right Honble the Lord Viscount Mandevill. Executor of the laft Will and Testament of the said Sir Nathaniel Riche as also in the presence of William Jesopp and Thomas Allaby Servants of the said Sr Nathaniel Riche give and bequeath unto the said William Jesopp all the adventure that he the said Sir Nathaniel Riche then had in the stock of the Company of Merchants of the City of London trading into the East-Indies— and he the said Sir Nathaniel Riche did also grant unto him the said William Jesopp the Tennancy of all that fferme lying in Stondon in the said Will menconed called Brooks Tenement which had been purchased by the said Sir Nathaniel Riche since his purchase of the Manor of Stondon The said William Jesopp paying for the same fforty shillings per annum and the Quitt Rent due from thence to the Mannor of Stondon aforesaid desiring the said Lord Viscount Mandevill to make a Lease thereof unto the said William Jessopp at at the Rents aforesaid And did further exprefs his intention to grant him interest in the said fferme upon the said Rents during the naturall life of the said Wm Jefsopp by saying that he would fayne have him the said William Jefsopp to live there and the said Sir Nathaniel Riche did also signify his Will to be that all the wearing apparell of him the said Sir Nathaniel Riche shall be distributed unto Mr Thomas Grimsditch in the said Will menconed and unto the said Thomas Allaby and William Jefsopp indifferently

Will proved 1st December 1636, by Edward Lord Viscount Mandevill before Thomas Eden and Henry Marten.

Thomas Welham

Deputy Register

Notes on the Will of Sir Nathl Rich

Jane the sister of Sir Nathl Rich married Thomas Grimsditch or Grymesditch. Their son Thomas was sent over to the Su‾mer Islands and their daughter Frances had been adopted by Sir Thomas & Dame Margaret Wroth, and lived in their household. In reference to the bequest of Sir Nathl to his sister Grymesditch, and its limitations, an appeal was made to the King for relief in the matter. "March 1638. Contents of the will of Sir Nathaniel Rich concerning his bequest to Thomas Grymesditch of seven shares in the Su‾mer Islands Company, on condition of residing there with his family within one year, also the King's letter excusing Grymsditch from doing so by reason of his continual attendance on his Majesty and the infirmity of his wife." John Grymsditch, a relation, was brother in law of Sir Francis Windebout, Foreign Secretary.

Viscount Mandeville was the eldest son of the 1st Earl of Manchester. He was impeached by the King before the Earl died in 1642, but it was dropped. He and John Pym were among the 6 members of the Houses impeached. He is known in the history of the Montagu family, as the "fighting Earl" who married 5 wives. One of them, was Lady Ann Rich daughter of the 2nd Earl of Warwick. He was a firm adherent of the Parliament, not so much as an opposer of the King, as an advocate of public rights. From Edgehill to Marston Moor and Newberry he appeared in every field, as Vic^t Mandeville or Earl of Manchester. He was universally beloved, his enemies rendering him every respect. He died in 1670.[x]

The Earl of Warwick (the Admiral) "He was a Man of a pleasant and companionable wit and conversation, of an universal Jollity and great Licence in his words and action, neverthelefs he had great authority and credit with his party and by opening his Doors and making his House the rendezvous of all silenced Ministers, in the time of their Misfortunes and spending a good part of his Estate upon them, he got the stile of a godly man." Edmund Calamy, in his funeral sermon applies to him what was said of Socrates "all who knew him, loved him, and if any man did not love him, 'twas because he did not know him." 'Tis supposed his death was hastened by that of his Grandson, for when the Funeral was delayed longer than he Expected, he was heard to say "if they staid a little longer, they should carry him down to be buried with him." And indeed he followed him in about 9 weeks time. Mr Knightly a gentleman of Northamptonshire, coming to Leighs,[A] his country seat and beholding the fine park and gardens, said pleasantly to him "my Lord you had need to make sure of Heaven or else when you die you will be a great Loser." The Grandson died of the Kings evil soon after his marriage (11 Nov

---

[x]Court from Queen Elizabeth to Queen Anne, by the Duke of Manchester.

[A]or Leige-

1657) to Frances the Protector's youngest Daughter. He died 16 Feb. 1657/8 & was buried March 5 at Felsted. He was a person of great hopes and when a youth of 13 or 14 years he carried himself with so much "civility, modesty, Ingenuity and Manlinefs as made him fit company for men. He had a strong persuasion in the height and vigor of his youth that he should not live beyond his mother's age who died under 27 and he under 24.[X]

The Earl of Warwick, was the friend and patron of Hugh Peters and like Sir Nathaniel Rich was greatly interested in the welfare of the New England settlements. In 1620, Nov[r] 3[d] a grant was issued "to Robert Earl of Warwick to be of the Council for the Plantation of New England."

Henry Rich, created Lord Kensington and Earl of Holland was brother to the Earl of Warwick. He married Isabel daughter of Sir Walter Cope who was a great promoter of the Virginia Company and a member of its governing Council. Isabel Cope brought into the Rich family the property in London, where Kensington Park now lies. In 1654 it was valued in the Afsefsors books at 640 £ per annum, these being in all, 408 acres with the Countefses house and gardens. In 1628 Henry Rich, 1st Earl of Holland was granted a pension of £2000 per annum He enjoyed it 21 years, at the end of which time he was beheaded. In the first year of pension, he was pressed for money and had his wife to write the following letter to Sir Nath[l] Rich "Sweet friend — You may justly accuse me for I condemn myself for incivility, that now may be thought to write rather out of necessity than affection. At this time indeed, ,my occasions are such that I must needs entreat you to be bound with Sir Robert Rich and M[r] Tompkins for 300£ or 400£ until my Lord's money come in

---

[X] Tindall's Essex -

wherein I would not trouble you but that I am confident you all know how to repay yourselves. I pray give me your answer with speed because the man from whom I should have it goeth out of town. I pray Excuse this boldness and let this assure you that there is none that wishes you more hearty love and affection than your faithful loving friend.[A]

I. Holland

Essex Rich, the daughter of Robert Rich, 1st Earl of Warwick and Penelope daughter of Walter Deveraux Earl of Essex. She married Sir Thomas Cheek K^{nt} of Pigo, and their daughter Essex, the widow of Sir Robert Bevill re-married Viscount Mandeville, after the death of his wife, her cousin, Lady Ann Rich. Robert Rich, 3rd Earl of Warwick (the Admiral) married as his second wife the sister of the above Essex Cheek — Ann Cheek the widow of _____ Rogers. They were married Oct 3^d 1645 at Whitehurst.

William Jessop mentioned in the will, was interested in the Summers Island and Providence Companies, and made the Treasurer. Under the Commonwealth he was one of the Clerks of the Privy Council.

Nathaniel Browne is supposed to have been the eldest son of the four children of Percy Browne, and after the premature death of both his parents, was adopted by his uncle, who placed him under the charge of the Revd Thomas Hooker. Whether he emigrated to New England with him in 1633, or was sent over the next year is not known, but the following letter of John Winthrop was no doubt in answer to one from Sir N^l Rich, making some enquiries, in reference to sending his nephew to the colony. —

[A] Court and Society from Queen Elizth to Anne by the Duke of Manchester.

John Winthrop to Sir Nathaniel Rich

Abstract   Boston Massachusetts, May 22^d - 1634.

The people of the Colony had not been formally numbered, by reason of "David's example" but were believed to be more than 4.000," in good health and for the most part well provided." There had been very little sickness or mortality "through the Lord's special providence." Provisions were for various seasons sufficient and plentiful. The winters were "sharp" but the summers were more "fervent in heat than in England." — "Our civil government is mixed. The freemen choose the magistrates every year (and for the present they have chosen Thomas Dudley Esqr Governor) and at four courts in the year, three out of each town (there being eight in all) do afsist the magistrates in making of laws imposing taxes, and disposing of lands. Our juries are chosen by the freemen of each town. Our churches are governed by pastors, teachers, and ruling elders and deacons, yet the power lies in the whole community and not in the presbytery, further than for order and precedency. For the natives, they are near all dead of the small pox, so as the Lord hath cleared our title to what we pofsess."

The letter concludes with an account of some violence offered to Lord Saye's men, who wished to trade, and some of whom lost their lives in the brawl. In a postscript it is added that six ships had arrived with passengers and cattle after six weeks' sail and that a plantation had been settled two hundred miles to the northward near Merrimac, of which Mr Parker was to be the minister.

Edmund Calamy preached the funeral sermon at the interment of Robt 2nd Earl of Warwick at Felsted Essex, which was published and dedicated to his son Robert, 3rd Earl.

Dame Margaret Wroth

Margaret Rich the sister of Sir Nathaniel Rich married Sir Thomas Wroth Knight. He was knighted by King James I[st] at Theobolds, 11th November 1613. The Wroths were neighbors of the King, at Wrothsplace, Enfield, Middlesex. They also had a place at Petherton Park, Somersetshire, and here Dame Margaret died in 1635 when Sir Thomas wrote a paper, entitled "his declaration of the life, sickness and death of his dearest and most beloved wife" and commenced it thus "At Petherton Park in the County of Somerset, Monday being the 6th of October 1635 about midnight of the same day Dame Margaret Wrothe my most sweet, most dear, most loving, most virtuous, most religious, most gracious, most discreet, merciful, patient humble and tender hearted wife of whom neither I nor the world was worthy, was taken with a sudden vomiting and sickness upon which followed a very hot fever with a great pain, which so tormented her that she often cried out, "the arrows of the Almighty are upon me, they stick fast in me." Sir Thomas adds "she wanted no attendance or comfort that could be procured for love or money: and I her husband take God, mine owne conscience, and all these good people who were there continually about her, that I omitted no duty of charge bodily pains, frequent prayers, sighs, groans and tears, to show my faithful and certain affection to her. Such was my high estimation of her worth and desire of her life, that if mine might have redeemed hers, I would have laid it down with ten thousand times more willingness than I was, or now am to survive her" She died on Wednesday the 14th of the month aged 55. "Divers years before her death she was daily and constantly conversant with God and frequent and constant in religious duties both private and public, making it her daily delight, slighting the things of this world much desiring and preparing hourly for her dissolution: much time she spent in prayer, reading the Bible or other good books and conference and discourse with good men & women, very discreet, prudent and active she was in the Conduct of her family, setting forward with her own hands divers works, and businesses in her house, always doing some good, protesting that she could not endure idlenefs and that she knew there was no warrant in the Word of God to be idle, for then Satan would be very busy with his detestable allurements and temptations and this divers can testify who were of her familiar acquaintance. Little speech she used in time of her sickness for in her health it was her wisdom to spare her tongue, but when she spake her words were gracious and discreet and to give her but her due, she was a woman adorned with as many singular parts and abilities pertaining to her sex and of as sweet a temper of spirit & constitution of body, as any man may Expect in a woman." Before the illness of Dame Margaret was considered hopeless, says Sir Thomas "being then in reasonable strength of mind, she called to me her husband and said "Let me kiss thee, sweetheart before I die" and so she did. The next day, after I her husband standing at her bedside both of us looking steadfastly one upon the other, I stooped down and kissed her wherefore she said "Do not make too much of me, lest it make me unwilling to die." At the beginning of her sicknefs she acquainted, her husband, how she had disposed of her land, jewels, money and other goods, which she and I her husband had agreed before she came out of London the last past summer committing her trust to me for the faithful Execution of her desires, contained in a will or Declaration she had made in writing under hand and seal and left with a worthy friend in London." She desired to be buried in the Church of St Stephen's Coleman St — that Church afterwards so famous for its undersexton John Haywood, who from the numerous alleys in that parish, in the great plague year, fetched the numerous dead from their houses in hand barrows carried them to his cart in waiting in the broader street and never had the distemper at all. Dame Margaret, Sir Thomas continues "further told me that she had entrusted her brother Sir Nathaniel Rich and myself with the education of her niece Frances a pretty and toward young child then waiting on her) desiring me for her sake to be very careful of her and said she had given her 100£ and some other things, if she took good courses to our liking. She asked those about her to "lift her up" and when they asked her "whether they should lift her"? She answered "to Christ." after recounting the past pious ejaculations and the final falling asleep the widower says "and I, most disconsolate man, a man of sorrows for the lofs of the wife of my bosom, the delight of my heart & chiefest comfort and content of my life, do most earnestly desire if it stand with the pleasure of my good God, so soon as I have seen the body of my dearest wife interred to be speedily dissolved and be with her in Paradise." He then composed the following, no doubt suggested by Sir Thomas Overbury's poem "a wife."

"Sir Thomas Wrothe, his sad encomium upon his dearest consort Dame Margaret Wrothe who died of a fever at Petherton Park in the County of Somerset, about midnight of the 14th day of October - 1635. -

> Can any sorrow be like mine, whose loss
> Is more than tongue may tell or heart conceive?
> Am I picked out to bear this heavy cross
> And in obedience, what is dearest leave?
> With bleeding heart I must avow, that no man
> Did ever lose more virtuous, worthy woman.

An angel's tongue were fitter than my pen
To blaze abroad her worth and virtues rare
She daily walked with God, more than with men
　　Yet men and women often had a share
Of her - - - from mouth and hand
And blest the house was where she did command.

　　A cheerful spirit and a patient, both
Her sweet composed body did possess
Neatness she highly prized and hated sloth,
　　As did her words and actions all Express
She had no warrant — often would she say
To spend a minute idle, of a day.

　　Gracious her words but few: small wrongs she had
them
The greatest injuries that e'er were done her
She did remit and nourished those who did them
　　So merciful she was, good words soon won her
There's not a heart that is not foul and rotten
Which loved not her, when that shall be forgotten.

　　Fit for his cabinet who now hath ta'en her
The world nor I was worthy for to share
　　So <u>Rich</u> a gem — but Heaven is now the gainer.
To sum up all, this woman, this my wife
She was the honour, comfort of my life.

If prayers incessant, from a bleeding heart

If sighs, heart rending groans and floods of tears
If gold and silver, or physycians art
    If merciful and helpful women's cares
Had been of force (with loss of my dear life)
They had redeemed from death, my dearer wife

But who can ransom or redeem his brother
From Death's impartial stroke? If any
    My part in this has been beyond all other
For by her death, my loss is more than many
But since it is decreed that all must die
All must submit to that — and so must I.

Yet this, Great God of Heaven, is my request
(Because I must without this comfort, live)
    Teach me to live as she did who is blest —
That I may die as she did — lastly — give
Thy servant leave to see her with his eyes
After this life — then happy when he dies.

Then follows a reference to her desire to be buried where her parents &
child were entombed and where says Sir Thomas quaintly,
        I will lie by thee, who lay by me
        For twenty years and one
and then concludes thus
        Rest then sweet woman, in that silent cell
        Until the resurection bring thee forth,
        Meanwhile, thy life these lines and tongues shall tell
        Thou wert a woman of a matchless worth

A pattern to all ladies who outlive thee

More would I say, if more praise I could give thee.

Abstract of Dame Margaret Wroths will —

Will made August 15th 1635. — Desires to be buried in the parish Church of St Stephans, Coleman Street London where her daughter Ann Bowdler is buried, and leaves 100 marks to be expended upon a monument for herself and her daughter. Mourning suits to be given to all these persons who attend her funeral — Sir Thomas Wroth and all the servants which shall serve him in the country, and in London, her dear brother Sir Nathaniel Rich the right honorable the Earl of Warwick and his countess, her loving brother in law Sir Peter Wroth and his wife, her sister Grimsditch and her husband, her worthy friend Mrs Moore, her "loving ffrende Mr Pheasant" Mr Sotherten — and their wives, Mr Slaughter, Mr John Pim and Mr Simons the pastor of Ironmonger Lane and his wife and her very good friend Mr Bower & his wife, Mr Goodwin the Minister of Coleman Street, and his wife, together with the clerke of the said parish, her godson Mr Richard St Pitty and his mother, Mrs Bassett and her daughter Mary, "who is lately marryed." She gives to Lady Mandeville a coronet of Goldsmith's work, her mother was her most deare and loving friend — the coronet was set with diamonds, rubies and pearls, "which sometime was Lady Mandevilles mothers." For her to "accept and weare the said coronet for my sake," To Frances daughter of her sister Frances Grimsditch three score and ten pounds to make up the 30£ which her daughter Ann Bowdler gave her by her last will, which 100£ she desires may be paid her on her marriage. To her good friend Mr Peter Pheasant, one diamond ring of the full value and worth of 10£ and to Mrs Mary Pheasant his wife she gives her gold ring set with seven diamonds "to weare for her sake." To the daughter of the said Mrs Mary Pheasant, who is her god daughter, her bracelet of gold with the amethyst stones and her bodkin together with the diamond button at the end of it and also her bracelets of pearls, and to her sister the wife of Mr John Sotherton she gives her great Sheet wrought all over with black silk and one pair of pillow "beares" soe wrought belonging to the said sheets" and also her waistcoat wrought with gold and silver which of them she pleases at her own choice and to the said Mr Sotherton her husband, she gives one ring of diamonds of the full worth & value of 10£. To her sister Grimsditch all her ordinary gowns & linnen. To Sir Peter Wroth a table diamond ring to weare for her sake, to Elizabeth Wroth, Sir Peter's eldest daughter 200£ To her nephew Thomas Grimsditch 5£ when he comes of age. She gives the above 200£ to Elizabeth Wroth as she had the education of her, and had taken a great fancy to her. To her nephew Robert Browne one share of the Somers Islands Company, she bought of one _____ Woodcocke, said share to be placed in trust of Mr John Sotherton, during her nephew's minority. A legacy is left to her worthy friend Mrs Moore— and 50£ to 50 poor women who are to attend her body to the grave, in mourning gowns provided at her expense. Her brother Sir Nathaniel Rich and Mr Peter Pheasant to be her Executors.

_____

Elizabeth Rich, sister of the above Dame Wroth was the fourth wife of Sir John Morgan Knight of Chilworth, near Albury, Surrey. Sir John was knighted for his services in the Expedition against Cadiz in 1596. He died 3^d April 1621 — She remarried John Sotherton Esqr Baron of the Exchequer, and died at Chilworth 30 November 1632. He remarried (see the will of Dame Margaret Wroth) a daughter of Mr Peter and Mary Pheasant.

_____

St Stephen's Church, Coleman Street London, was burnt in the great fire. Dame Margaret Wroth left to this church the sum of two pounds yearly to preach a sermon on the recurrence of her funeral day, being November 11th, and after each sermon Two pounds to be paid to the poor. She also gave £1.0.0 to be paid yearly for a sermon to be preached on the Funeral day of her daughter Mrs Anna Bowdley, and after each sermon, to the poor £1.0.0.

At the time of Dame Margaret Wroths death the Revd John Goodwin was the clergyman of the Coleman Street Church to which living he had been presented in 1633. He became a zealous supporter of Armenianism, and should not be confounded with the Revd Thomas Goodwin, who was also a friend of the Rich family, particularly of Sir Nathaniel, who is alluded to in some of Dr Goodwin's works.

Brownes of Snelston - Derbyshire

Thomas Browne ═══ Margaret, daughter to ____ Chatham, of the family of Chatham of
of Snelston, C° Derby   Chatham near Manchester & related to Humphrey Chatham founder of the
                            Cheatham Free Library & Blue Coat School of Manchester

Nicholas Browne ═══ Elianor dᵣ & heiress to Ralph Shirley Esq of Shirley, Derbyshire,
of Snelson– Buried   & Staunton– Harold & Braylesford C° Leicester. Her first husband
Janᵞ 18th 1587.   was Thomas Vernon 2nd son of Humphrey Vernon of Clifton &
His wife died April   Harleston Derbyshire, as by the marriage settlement made 1545
18th. 1595.   May 5. The Shirleys of Shirley & of Staunton Harold were
                         represented in 1611 by a Baronet in 1677 by Baron Ferrar & in
                         1711 by Earl Ferrars of Staunton Harold.

Thomas
Browne died
without issue

Rodulphus Browne
also a son Ralphe
who was buried
April 18th 1577

Sir William Browne ———— Mary Savage Born in ———— Gertrude Browne
Germany. Naturalized in
1600

Sir William Browne
born in 1558 at Snelston.
Served for several years in
the Low Counries and died
there in 1610, August. Was
Lieu^t Governor of
Flushing.

William Browne
died young, but
naturalized by
Act of
Parliament 1604
Baptized Nov
10th 1594

Ann Browne
died young
naturalized by
act of Parliament
1604

Barbara Browne
died an infamt
but natz^d 1604

Percy Browne, ———— Rich
natz^d 1622 born   daughter of Col
about 1602   Nathl Rich of
                        Standon Essex
                        died before 1635

Mary Browne Born in Holland,
natz^d 1622

Nathaniel Browne sent
over to New England under
the charge of the Rev^d
Thomas Hooker about
1633-4. M^d in New
England & had 10 Sons.

Robert Browne went to the Providence
Islands, West Indies - named after Robert
Sydney Earl of Leicester was ordained a
minister and appointed to a church in
Somers Islands in 1655 and died there in
1660.

Samuel Browne

Browne educated by the Countess
of Leicester widow of Robert Sydney,
1st Earl of Leicester of the Sydney
family. His name supposed to be
William as a Wm Browne was out in the
Providence Islands

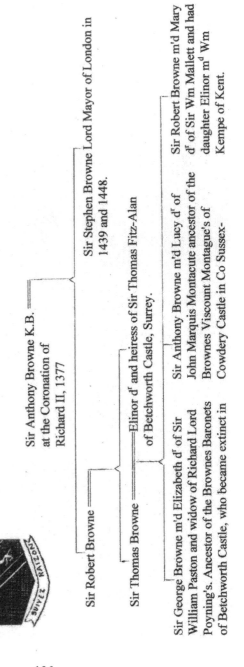

Browne - Mss. Coll. Arms - Vincent Surrey No 129

Sir Anthony Browne K.B. at the Coronation of Richard II, 1377

Sir Robert Browne

Sir Thomas Browne = Elinor dᵃ and heiress of Sir Thomas Fitz-Alan of Betchworth Castle, Surrey.

Sir Stephen Browne Lord Mayor of London in 1439 and 1448.

Sir George Browne m'd Elizabeth dᵃ of Sir William Paston and widow of Richard Lord Poyning's. Ancestor of the Brownes Baronets of Betchworth Castle, who became extinct in

Sir Anthony Browne m'd Lucy dᵃ of John Marquis Montacute ancestor of the Brownes Viscount Montague's of Cowdery Castle in Co Sussex-

Sir Robert Browne m'd Mary dᵃ of Sir Wm Mallett and had daughter Elinor mᵈ Wm Kempe of Kent.

Stowe, in his "Survey of London" says of the above Sir Stephen Browne that he was Lord Mayor of London in 1439 and again in 1448, having been Sheriff in 1431. He further says that he was the son of John Browne of New Castle upon Tyne. Amongst the "Honourable acts of Citizens" Stowe records that "Stephen Browne, Grocer Mayor in 1439 sent into Prussia, causing corn to be brought from thence to London in great quantities whereby he brought down the price of wheat from three shillings the bushel to lefs than half that money / for corn was then so scarce in England that poor people were enforced to make their Bread of Fern roots." For this praiseworthy act, he no doubt received the order of Knighthood, with perhaps some augmentation of the family arms granted in 1377, which so closely resemble those borne by the Brownes of Snelston at Gilbert Dethick's (Garter King at Arms) visitation of Debyshire, in 1569, that it would seem the latter were derived from them. The principal difference is in the crest; that of the Brownes of Eastbourne (Vic't Montague's) and the Bechworth family being "an eagle displayed, vert," whilst the Brownes of Snelston bore as crest "an eagle's head erased sable & gorged." Sir Anthony Browne (1377) was in all probability, not the father, as Vincent states but the grandfather of Sir Stephen Browne, Lord Mayor.

Concerning Sir Stephen Browne, Fuller adds a few other particulars, "that during a great dearth in his Mayorality, he charitably relieved the wants of the poor citizens by sending ships at his own expense to Dantzic which returned laden with rye and which seasonable supply soon sunk grain to reasonable rates. He is beheld as one of the first merchants, who during a want of corn, shewed the Londoners the way to the barn door, I mean Spurred and, prompted by Charity (not covetousnefs) to this adventure." The above pedigree is taken from

Dallaway's Sussex108 — and differs from Heath's History of the Grocer's Company of London. Heath gives Sir Stephen Browne a different coat of arms from the above. Stow's Survey of London gives Sir Stephen — John as his father and says he was from New Castle. It will be observed there is a period of 70 years between Sir Stephen & his reputed father in Vincent's pedigree.

Stowe, gives a list of Lord Mayors of London who were Grocers and the names of those Ex-Lord Mayors who died and were buried in some of the London churches. The name of Sir Stephen Browne does not occur among those named as having died in London, and we may conclude that after 1448 he withdrew from the city with his family and settled in Derbyshire at or near Snelston. This would tally with the tradition handed down from the original progenitor of the Browne family in New England "that they were descendants of a Sir Stephen Browne in England." Descendants of the Brownes of the Eastbourne branch can be traced in New England by the arms they bore. In the "Heraldic Journal of American Families" Vol 3 page 14 is found the copy of an inscription on the tombstone of the Revd Marmaduke Brown, at Newport R.I with an engraved coat of arms, similar to those borne by Vic^t Montagu & the Brownes of Betchworth Castle. The family of this Marmaduke Brown it is stated, came originally from Ireland. In England it is mentioned that "a branch of the Brownes of Kiddington & Caversham of Oxfordshire (offshoots of the Eastbourne family at Cowdrey Castle) according to an uncertain tradition was settled in Ireland in 1565, the ancestor having accompanied Sir Henry Sydney (father of Sir Philip & Sir Robert) Lord Deputy, from whom the present Marquis of Sligo, is descended." Again we find some inscriptions copied from a graveyard in Salem, New England, (Vol 2 page 23 of the Heraldic Journal) to William Brown Esq & his wife Sarah with the Brown arms and crest. The crest is that of the

Brownes of Eastbourne & Betchworth, whilst on a bend between 2 Cottises, argent, are 3 Eagles displayed, which is probably a mistake, and should be 3 lions passant — for it is mentioned that the gravestone inscriptions "are very imperfect" and it may be also inferred that the eagles would be but imperfectly and incorrectly decyphered, in the worn state of the stone.

The Family of Rich

"Randell Surnamed ye Rich, a Norman borne had issue 1st Simon, Count Lize and Earl of Huntingdon by marrying of Maud daughter of Waltheof Earl of Northumberland and Earl of Huntingdon. 2nd Warner le Rich his brother, both marched and came into England to ye aide of William the Conqueror and brought with them 40 knights. Simon had Simon Rich Kn^t, Earl of Huntingdon anno 1184. 31. Henry 2^d. Sir Edmund Rich and Mable his wife had issue Sir Edmund Rich dead in 1240. 2^d Sir Robt Rich borne in Abingdon Berkshire, as his brother Sir Edmund, he dyed 1250. 3^d Margaret Rich and 4th, Alice Rich both at Abingdon and successively priorefses of Catesby Northamptonshire — the first dyed in 1257 the second Alice dyed in 1270. Sr Edmund hall, Oxford had its name from Sr Edmund Rich, who was first Canon of Salisbury, and then Archbishop of Canterbury. He dyed at Soissons France in 1240, his brother Robert wrote his life. A branch of this family settled in Hampshire, where John le Rich flourished at Rich's place about the time of Edward the 2d. His great grandson Richard Rich Esquire was of London and died in the year 1414.

The metrical narrative of Robert Rich was the first printed account of the wreck of the "Sea Venture." The play of the "Tempest" is supposed to have been the latest composition of Shakespeare, and to have had much of its local colouring, suggested by the circumstances of the wreck on the "vexed Bermoothes," which would be much talked of at the time. The Earl of Southampton, the friend of Shakespeare, was at that time on friendly terms with Sir Nathaniel Rich the brother of Robert. The Earl who was one of the foremost men in the management of the Virginia Comp^y in which Sir Nathaniel was also much interested, would be disposed to talk much about the wreck & it is not unlikely that Robert Rich would be much questioned, and frequently asked for the narrative of his Experience, and it may be in Shakespeares presence. The copy of Rich's tract "Newes from Virginia," was found in the library of the Earl of Charlemont in Dublin in 1865 by John O Halliwell-Phillips Esq, who printed an edition privately of 25 copies, of which 15 were destroyed, leaving only 10 for distribution. In 1613 was also published in London "A plaine description of the Barmudas now called Sommer Ilands. With the manner of their discoverie Anno 1609 by the shipwrack & admirable deliverance of Sir Thos Gates & Sir George Sommers, wherein are truly set forth the Commodities & profits of that Rich, Pleasant & Healthfull Countrie with an Addition, or more ample relation of divers other remarkable matters concerning those Ilands, since then Experienced, lately sent thence by one of the Colonists now resident there." Ecclesiastes. 3.11 "God hath made every thing beautifull in his time." Dedicated to Sir Thos Smith & with an "Epistle Dedicatorio" by W. C. (William Crankshaw, D. D.)

Newes from Virginia

The Lost Flocke Triumphant:

With the happy Arrival of that famous and

worthy Knight Sr Thomas Gates: and

His well reputed and valient Cap-

tanie Mr Christopher New-

porte, and others, into

England.

With the manner of their distresse in the Land of Devils,

(otherwise called Barmoothawes) where they

remayned 42 weekes, and builded

two Pynaces, in which

they returned into Virginia

By R. Rich, Gent, one of the voyage

London

Printed by Edw. Allde and are to be solde by John

Wright, at Christ-Church dore. 1610.

To the Reader.

Reader, — how to stile thee I knowe not, perhaps learned,

111

perhaps unlearned; happily captious, happily envious: indeed, what or how to tearme thee I know not, only as I began I will proceede.

Reader: Thou dost peradventure imagine that I am mercenarie in this business and write for money (as your moderne Poets are) hyred by some of those ever to be admired adventurers to flatter the world. No; I disclaime it. I have knowne the voyage, past the danger, seene that honorable work of Virginia and I thanke God am arrived here to tell thee what I have seene, don, and past. If thou wilt believe me, so; if not, so to: for I cannot force thee but to thy owne liking. I am a soldier, blunt and plaine, and so is the phrase of my newes; and I protest it is true. If thou aske why I put it in verse, I prithee knowe it was only to feede mine owne humour. I must confess, that, had I not debarde myselfe of that large scope which to the writing of prose is allowed, I should have much easd myself and given thee better content. But I intreat thee to take this as it is, and before many daies expire, I will promise thee the same work more at large.

I did feare prevention by some of your writers, if they should have gotten but some part of the newes by the tayle, and therefore though it be rude, let it passe with thy liking, and in so doing I shall like well of thee; but, however, I have not long to stay. If thou wilt be unnaturall to thy country man, thou maist — I must not loose my patrymonie. I am for Virginia againe, and so I will bid the hartily farewell with an honest voice:

As I came hether to see my native land,

To waft me backe lend me thy gentle hand.

Thy loving country-man

R. R.

Newes from Virginia
of the happy arrival of that famous
and worthy knight Sir
Thomas Gates
and well reputed and valiante Captaine
Newport, into England.

———

"It is no idle fabulous tale,
Nor is it fayned newes
For Truth herself is heere arriv'd
Because you should not muse.
With her both Gates and Newport come,
To tell Report doth lye,
which did devulge into the world,
That they at sea did dye.

Tis true that eleaven monthes and more
These gallant worthy nights
was in the shippe Sea-Venture nam'd,
Deprived Virginia's sight:
and bravely did they glyde the maine
Till Neptune 'gan to frowne
As if a courser proudly backt
would throwe his ryder downe.

The seas did rage, the windes did blowe
Distressed were they then;
Their shippe did leake, her tacklings breake,
In daunger were her men,

But heaven was pylotte in this storme
And to an iland nere
Bermooth was called, conducted them
which did abate their feare.

But yet these worthies forced were
Opprest with weather againe
To runne their ship between two rockes
Where she doth still remaine;
And then on shoare the island came
Inhabited by hogges
Some foule, and tortoyses there were
They onley had one dogge.

To kille these swyne to yield them foode
That little had to eate
Their store was spent, and all things scant
Alas! they wanted meate.
A thousand hogges that dogge did kill
Their hunger to sustaine
And with such foode, did in that ile
Two and forty weekes remaine,

And there two gallant pynases
Did build of seader-tree
The brave Deliverance one was call'd
Of seaventy tunne was shee
The other Patience had to name
Her burthen thirty tunne

114

Two only of their men which there
Pale death did overcome.

And for the losse of these two soules
Which were accounted deere
A son and daughter then was borne
And were baptized there.
The two and forty weekes being past
They hoyst sayle and away;
Their ships with hogs well freighted were
Their harts with mickle joy.

And so to Virginia came
Where these brave soldiers finde
The English-men opprest with griefs
And discontent in minde;
They seem'd distracted and forlorne
For those two worthies' losse,
Yet at their home returne, they joye'd
Amongst them some were crosse.

And in the midst of discontent,
Came noble Delaware;
And heard the griefes, on either part
And set them free from care;
He comforts them, and cheers their hearts
That they abound with joy;
He feedes them full, and feedes their soules,
With God's word every day.

A discreet counsell he creates
Of men of worthy fame
That noble Gates, leiftenant was
The admiral had to name
The worthy Sir George Somers Knight
And others of command
Maister George Pearcy, which is brother
Unto Northumberland.

Sir Fardinando Wayneman, Knight
And others of good fame
That noble lord his company
Which to Virginia came
And landed there, his number was
One hundred seaventy; then
ad to the rest, and they make full
Foure hundred able men.

Where they unto their labour fall
As men that mean to thrive.
Let's pray that heaven may bless them all
And keep them long alive
Those men that vagrants liv'd with us
Have these deserved well,
Their governour writes in their praise
As divers letters tel.

And to the adventurers then he writes

Be not dismayed at all
For scandall cannot doe us wrong
God will not let us fall.
Let England knowe our willingnesse
For that our worke is good
Wee hope to plant a nation
Where none before hath stood.

To glorifie the Lord 'tis done
And to no other end
He that would crosse so good a worke
To God can be no friend:
There is no feare of hunger here
For corne much store here growes
Much fish the gallant rivers yield
'Tis truth, without suppose.

Great store of fowle, of venison
Of grapes and mulberries
Of chestnuts, walnuts and such like
Of fruits and strawberries,
There is indeed no want at all
But some, condicion'd ill
That wish the worke should not goe on
With words doe seeme to kill.

And for an instance of their store
The Noble Delaware
Hath for a present hither sent

To testifie his care

In managing so good a worke

Two gallant ships, by name

The Blessing and the Hercules

Well fraught, and in the same

Two ships are these commodities

Furres, sturgeon, caviare

Black walnut-tree, and some deale boards

With such they laden are;

Some pearle, some wainscot and clapboards

With some sasafras wood

And iron promis't for 'tis true

Their mynes are very good.

Then maugre, scandall, false report

Or any opposition,

Th' adventurers doe thus devulge

To men of good condition,

That he that wants shall have reliefe

Be he of honest minde,

Apparel, Coyne, or anything

To such they will be kinde.

To such as to Virginia

Do purpose to repaire;

And when that they shall hither come

Each man shall have his share,

Day wages for the laborer

And for his more content,
A house and garden plot shall have
Beside 'tis further ment

That every man shall have apart,
And not thereof denied
Of generall profit, as if that he
Twelve pounds, ten shillings paid:
And he that in Virginia
Shall copper coyne receive
For hyer, or commodities,
And will the country leave

Upon delivery of such coyne
Unto the Governour
Shall by exchange, at his returne
Be by their treasurer
Paid him in London, at first sight
No man shall cause to grieve
For 'tis their general will and wish
That every man shall live.

The number of adventurers
That are for this plantation
Are full eight hundred worthy men
Some noble, all of fashion;
Good, discreete, their work is good
May heaven assist them in their worke
And then our newes is done."

119

Grant of Arms to the Summer Islands Company

John Burrough Knight of the Garter, grants the following arms to the "Governor & Company of the City of London for the Plantacon of the Summer Islands" at the instance of the Earl of Dorset Govr, Richard Caswell, Deputy & Anthony Peniston Treas^r — to wit "Argent, a Shipp in a wrought sea, wrecked between two Rocks, all proper & for their crest, upon a Helme & a torce of Argent & gules, a Bore on a Mount between two Palmetts, proper and alsoe two Tritons for their supporters" — 4th day August — 1635. —

INDEX OF PERSONS

Browne, Sir Anthony 6, 106, 107

Browne, Sir George 106

Browne, Sir Robert 106

Browne, Sir Stephen 106, 107, 108

Browne, Sir Thomas 105, 106

Browne, Sir William 1, 2, 4, 5, 11-61, 78, 105

Browne, Stephen 4

Browne, Thomas 104

Browne, William 105

Browne. Nicholas 104

Bucenvall, 38

Buckhurst, Lord Treasurer 26

Buckingham, Duke of 70, 73

Budley, Capt. 21

Burnham, Capt. 18

Burrough, John 120

Butler, Capt. Nathaniel 64

Calamy, Edmund 91, 94

Carlton, Sir Dudley 63

Caswell, Richard (see Earl of Dorset) 120

Cavendish, Lord 64

Cecil, Cecill, Sir Robert (or Mr. Secretary) 12, 16, 24, 25,26, 27, 28, 30, 36, 38, 41, 47, 52, 54.

Cecil, Sir Edward 68

Chaderton, Dr. 67

Chamberlain, John 63, 64

Champemon, Arthur 21

Chapman, Sir Peter 63

Charlemont, Earl of 110

Charles I 60, 71, 73, 81, 90

Charles IX of Sweden 53

Chatham, ___ 104

Chatham, Margaret 104

Cheek, ___ Ann 93

Cheek, Lady Essex 87

Cheek, Sir Thomas 93

Clarendon, Lord 72

Clark, Sir William 36

Clarke, Edward 70

Clarke, Mr. 72

Clasken, Sir William 40

Claypole, John 81

Coke, Sir Edward 63, 71, 73

Collins, Arthur 7, 11, 17, 48, 53

Compton, Lord 17

Cope, Isabel 92

Cope, Sir Walter 92

Coulton, Sir Dudley 64

Cradock, Mathew 62

Cramburne, Lord 52

Crankshaw, Rev. William 110

Cromwell, Oliver 59, 81

Cumberland, Earl of 21

Cuntstable, Mr. 42, 46

Dallaway, Rev. James 107

Danyell, Mr. 41

Darby, Lady of 54

Dean, J. W. 8

Delaware, Lord 77

Denmark, King of 52

Dethick, Gilbert 107

Deveraux, Penelope 63, 93

Deveraux, Walter 93

Devonshire, Countess of 68

Diggs, Sir Dudley 70, 71, 72, 73

Dockrey, Harry Knight 24

Dorset, Earl of (see Caswell) 120

Duckinfield, Col. 81

Dudley Family 5

Dudley, Robert (See Earl of Leicester) 52

Dudley, Thomas 94

Dugdale (King's Herald) 16

Durham, Thomas 74

Durham, Thomas 75

Eden, Thomas 90

Edmonds, Mr. 41

Edmonds, Sir Thomas 14, 56, 57, 59, 60

3

Rolf, John 63
Rolfe, Bermuda 76
Roth, Margaret (Rich) 1
Rudd, Mary 83
Rudd, Mathew 83
Ruddale, Richard 21
Rushforth 72
Russell, Francis 59
Russell, John 59
Russell, Sir William 14, 56, 57, 59, 78
Rutland, Lord 20, 27
Sackville, Edward 64
Salisbury, Marquiss of 16, 51
Sancroft, Dr. Wm. 65, 66
Sandys, Sir Edwin 64
Savage, Mary 13, 105
Saye, Lord 94
Scull, Edith 3
Scull, Gideon Delaplaine 2, 3, 5, 6, 10
Scull, Walter 3
Semer, Mr. 75
Shakespeare, William 2, 4, 76, 109, 110
Shirley, Antony 21, 22
Shirley, Ralph 104
Shirley. Elianor 104
Shrewsbury, Earl of 54
Sidney (see also Sydney) 5, 26
Sidney, Jack 19
Simons, Rev. 100
Slaughter, Mr. 100
Sligo, Marquis of 108
Smith, Dick 28
Smith, Smyth Sir John 14, 85
Smith, Smyth, Sir Thomas 14, 15, 64, 77, 78, 110
Somers, Sommers, Summers Sir George 74, 76, 77, 110, 116
Sotherton, John 100, 101
Southampton Earl of 23, 64, 77, 110

St. Pitty, Richard 100
Standen, Sir Anthony 48
Story,___ 9
Stowe, John 107, 108
Sweden, King of (Charles IX) 53
Sydney, Jack 22
Sydney, Lord 49
Sydney, Mary 26, 27, 50
Sydney, see also Sidney
Sydney, Sir Henry 108
Sydney, Sir Philip 11, 12, 28, 108
Sydney, Sir Robert 11, 12, 14, 15, 16, 17, 18, 23, 24, 25, 26, 28, 36, 42, 50, 53, 56, 57, 59, 61, 78 (and also often addressed as "My Lord," etc., in Sir William's letters, instead of by name.)
SydneyArthur , Lady 17
Taverner, Mr. R. 5
Thomas, Lord 20, 23
Thorneback, Col. Robert 82
Throckmorton, John 13, 17, 53
Tindall, W. 92
Tompkins, Mr. 92
Trumbull, William 5
Tucker, Daniel 64
Tuston, Ed 15
Uvedale, Edward 12
Valck, Mr. 43, 44, 46
Vanderwerck 44, 45, 46
Vane 81
Vavasour, Knight 24
Vere, Geoffrey 49
Vere, Mr. 38
Vere, Sir Francis 18, 24, 37, 41, 42, 49, 51, 59
Vere, Sir Horatio 48
Vere, Sir Horatio 49, 78
Vernon, Humphrey 104
Vernon, Thomas 104

6

Made in the USA
San Bernardino, CA
05 June 2018